GOZNEY°

Pizza
Volume 01

A guide to your pizza-making journey & other outdoor recipes

HarperCollins*Publishers*

HarperCollins*Publishers*
1 London Bridge Street
London SE1 9GF

www.harpercollins.co.uk

HarperCollins*Publishers*
Macken House, 39/40 Mayor Street Upper
Dublin 1, D01 C9W8, Ireland

First published by HarperCollins*Publishers* 2024

7 9 10 8 6

A catalogue record of this book is available from the British Library

ISBN 978-0-00-864094-1

Printed by GPS Group in Bosnia and Herzegovina.

This book contains FSC™ certified paper and other controlled sources to ensure responsible forest management.

For more information visit: www.harpercollins.co.uk/green

WHEN USING KITCHEN APPLIANCES PLEASE ALWAYS
FOLLOW THE MANUFACTURER'S INSTRUCTIONS

Introduction 38

01

Knowledge
14

02

Ingredients
24

03

Dough
36

04

Sauces, Dips & Toppings
80

Pizza
108

Outdoor
188

Index

Contributors

Acknowledgements

Introduction

Meet Tom Gozney.

———————————

Cooking with fire unites two basic elements: food and fire.

But the combination is so much more than just sustenance and heat. It's an experience that brings people together and unlocks so many opportunities for self-discovery.

My mother always said, when you're with a fire you're never alone. Perhaps it's a throwback to our ancestral past that we connect with. Or maybe it's some form of escapism from the fast-paced nature of modern living, where convenience and speed seem to be all too often prioritised.

There's just something that feels so instinctual about it. It can be enthralling and unpredictable. Maybe it's the danger of it or watching ingredients cook in seconds that's so appealing.

It's that magic that drew me in and started me on my journey.

'I threw myself into food. Cooking with fire was
something I could lose myself in. Better myself
at. It was a skill to master and a whole new way
of connecting with the people around me.'

Our History

In my early years I was always a timid, sensitive kid but when I started school, I really began to struggle. Unbeknownst to me, I had dyslexia. I knew I was capable, but not being able to learn in the same textbook way slowly eroded my self-esteem and I began acting out through frustration. I adopted this class clown persona that wasn't me, but it gave me the external validation I desperately craved. When I was thirteen, I was introduced to a friend group outside of school that were smoking and using drugs and it just felt like a natural progression for the persona I had embraced. Drugs and alcohol became intertwined in my perception of who I was. Over my teenage years this escalated, until at twenty-one I finally hit rock bottom, came to terms with my addiction and entered rehab.

Leaving treatment and returning home sober was the hardest thing I've ever done. I didn't want my sobriety to define me or stop me from hanging out with my friends but as much as I didn't want to admit it, I was struggling to be in social situations where everyone was drinking.

Fortunately, a year later I met my wife, Laura. I enjoyed cooking for her, and it sparked something: there was something in the ritual of it I could just lose myself in. I started having my mates over for dinners, and one night we made pizza. Unlike other dinners, everyone rolled up their sleeves and got involved. I witnessed this insane sense of community and connection. It felt special. But the pizza, cooked in a conventional oven, was shit.

I was inspired. The only problem was, we had no cash. I had been working as a labourer, and Laura was fresh out of university taking temporary contracts where she could. We were living on baked beans, pay cheque to pay cheque. Online you could only buy these expensive Italian imported pizza ovens that we would have never been able to afford, so I decided I would build my own.

Three days later we had a large, monstrous brick oven in our garden. It took 6 hours to get the beast up to temperature, but I loved every tinkering moment of it. It allowed me to socialise without alcohol being the focus. Instead of bringing tequila, my mates brought toppings, and everyone got involved. The oven became a conversation point with everyone 'having a go' at spinning pizzas.

Word got out. I started to build pizza ovens for friends and family, improving my designs as I built them, then broke into building brick ovens for pubs and restaurants. It was hard work. Variable concrete setting times, plummeting winter temperatures, lime burns, rain, pushing wheelbarrows of fire bricks on and off sites, and driving all over the UK.

One day, after a conversation with my brother-in-law, Geoff, I had a revelation. What if, instead of a hand-built brick oven, which was costly and so time intensive to build, I designed a pre-cast oven, which could be shipped to gardens all over the UK? The Stone Bake Oven Company was born.

I researched all there was to know about refractory materials and the size and shape of pizza ovens. My mother lent me five thousand pounds and I used it to make a mould and launch my first website.

Our ovens were the first of their kind in the market. Laura started to work with me, and we used to sell our ovens based on her hand-drawn sketches. People thought this was the brand's 'style', but the truth was we didn't have any photos of our product! We had modest expectations at the start. It was hard work convincing people they needed a pizza oven; many didn't know what a pizza oven even was at that point. It was months before we gave ourselves a pay cheque and years before we ever took a day off.

A movement started happening, with pizza ovens becoming more and more popular in the UK. Competitors began emerging so we made the decision to knuckle down and continue to focus on innovation, design and performance, values that would later become a backbone for the business. We re-branded to Gozney as it seemed more grown-up and reflected all the things we had learnt along the way. But my end goal stayed the same: I wanted to change the way the world cooked outdoors and make cooking with fire easier to get into. To do that we needed to make something smaller, more portable, more accessible.

Roccbox was born. Roccbox was the world's first stone-floored portable pizza oven. It changed the game. Distilling the design of our restaurant ovens into something more compact and portable enabled people to create pizza at home – or anywhere, really. Roccbox captured the hearts (and stomachs) of chefs, home cooks and design enthusiasts alike.

Since then, we have continued to push the boundaries of design and outdoor cooking. The Dome launched in 2021 and redefined the category. To date it is the greatest expression of who I am as a designer. It was like nothing else on the market. Its inspired aesthetic made it a true centerpiece to any garden, and it worked better and did so much more than any pizza oven before.

We've been on a pizza rocket ship ever since.

Why this book?

We haven't done a cookbook before. And we've always wanted to.

We have had a ton of cookbook ideas over the years, but they kept getting shelved for one reason or another. Truth be told we were obsessed with perfection, so obsessed we didn't know where to start. So, we've stripped it back to what really matters, paying attention to our community and our favourite tips and tricks, creating a simple, useful cookbook on pizza.

I'm not a chef, I'm just a passionate home cook. These recipes are how I like to cook, taking simple provisions and unlocking flavour with fire.

I love food made for sharing. All the recipes here have a short(ish) list of ingredients and reflect what I want to cook and eat. Some recipes are linked to dishes and experiences I had while building Gozney, and others are inspired by the phenomenal culinary trailblazers that I am fortunate enough to call friends.

I hope this cookbook makes you fall in love with the magic of cooking with fire and helps you learn the art of pizza. It can be as simple or complex as you'd like to make it. Just get the ingredients, light the oven and get out there.

I want this book to help you on your own journey of pizza and cooking with fire, whether you are new to pizza or just looking for some new recipe inspiration. There isn't anything better than getting your hands into flour and learning through trial and error. To give you the confidence, to not be afraid to try. It means so much to me for others to experience that sense of discovery and fulfillment that comes with the 'pizza life'.

Much love,
– Tom

01 Knowledge

Why Do I Need a Pizza Oven?

If you want to make restaurant-worthy pizza at home, you need a pizza oven. There are two reasons why you wouldn't just use a conventional oven like the ones we all have sitting in our kitchens today.

First, there's the functional, practical cooking performance aspect. Pizza is meant to be cooked in a specific environment; other methods are merely compromises. Yes, you can cook pizza in a home oven, but the pizza is never as good as it is coming out piping hot from a pizza oven. That's why restaurant pizza is so good.

A good pizza oven gets hot and stays hot, reaching up to 500°C (950°F). This creates a unique cooking environment. A rolling flame curls across the dome-shaped ceiling, designed to create the right movement of heat around the interior space, pushing the heat down into the stone floor. The floor absorbs the heat so food is hit with heat from all angles – top, bottom and reflected off the sides – giving you a consistent cook. The combination of fire, hot air and a hot stone reaches higher temperatures than any typical grill or home oven. And pizza ovens are highly insulated with a specific geometry of design, so they stay hot for a long night of slinging in pizza after pizza.

It's all about the high heat for pizza. When a pizza is launched into a pizza oven, the high heat of the air inside the oven and the heat emitted from the stone floor causes moisture to evaporate and carbon dioxide within the dough to expand. The porous stone floor sucks moisture out of the dough. When the pizza hits the stone floor the dough expands and gives rise to the crust. This is called 'oven spring'. The pizza oven cooks the pizza evenly and quickly, creating a crisp crust on the top and bottom, with a soft, airy interior.

Delicious. The experience of cooking with high heat goes beyond pizza. How the rolling flame renders the fat on meat and perfectly chars vegetables is unparalleled. The food you create becomes exceptional.

Second, is the experience. Cooking with a live fire at high temperatures makes for an active cook. Pizza cooks fast. Neapolitan pizza cooks in about 60 seconds. You can't set it and forget it; you get to be involved. The pizza launches and the action starts, with flames and rising dough – you have to keep a close eye while turning the pizza for a great bake. You become highly connected to the process. The flame is mesmerising. A pizza oven draws people in. Everyone becomes involved – prepping the toppings, opening up the dough or operating the oven. The oven enhances social connection and lets you interact with others around you in a new way. Phones are put down. Conversation picks up. Everyone wants to get in on the action. A pizza oven allows people who don't see themselves as creative to become creators.

In this book we've tried to give you enough tools and knowledge to either begin or elevate your pizza journey with a range of recipes from making dough to proven combinations of toppings on a spectrum of pizza styles. There's also some non-pizza, outdoor cooking recipes for those rare days you don't want pizza. Enjoy.

Essential Pizza Equipment & Tools

A not-so-secret secret to making great pizza is having the right tools for the job. These are essential for creating and crafting. It's more than an oven, dough and ingredients. Start your pizza journey with the proper equipment.

Peels: Turning and Placement

Launch, place, maneuver and turn. A placement peel – made from metal or wood – is essential for getting pizza into and out of the oven. Wood is good for beginners and others who like to build their pizzas right on the peel, metal is easier to wield and great for sliding under a pie made on a work surface, and often has perforations in the blade to let extra flour sift through before launching the pizza into the oven. The turning peel slides under your pizza while it's in the oven so you can pivot and rotate it for an even cook.

Dough Cutter and Dough Scraper

Cutter: an essential tool for portioning your dough. Cut, shape and divide your dough into dough ball portions.

Scraper: a handy tool to manage and move dough from bowl to worktop, and especially helpful for high hydration doughs.

Pizza Cutter

Essential for slicing your pizzas without disturbing your toppings. The traditional wheel cutter rolls through the pizza. The rocker, or mezzaluna, rocks through your pizza. Whichever cutter you choose, opt for a good-quality sharp tool that will enable you to slice effortlessly. When using your cutter, a single swift motion is recommended for that clean cut.

Digital Kitchen Scale

Essential for measuring the right amount of flour, yeast, salt and water. We recommend both precision scales with accuracy to 0.01 gram, for salt and yeast, and a scale with accuracy to 1 gram for weighing other ingredients. We recommend weighing in metric, as it's more accurate than imperial or cups and helpful for proportions.

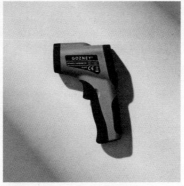

Infrared Thermometer

Different styles of pizza like different cooking temperatures. Knowing and monitoring the heat of your oven helps you know when you're ready to start cooking pizza as well as maintaining the right cooking temperatures. A handheld infrared thermometer will give you an accurate reading of the oven-floor temperature.

Measuring Cup

Great pizza is all about great pizza dough. Accurate and consistent measurement is key. A measuring cup is a great vessel to use alongside your kitchen scales. Being specific about the amount of water is crucial when making pizza dough.

Dough Tray

Keep your dough in the right environment for proofing in an airtight container/tray, which acts as easy dough storage in the fridge for cold fermenting.

Bowls and Cups

There's going to be a lot of mixing, sorting and combining in your future. Keep your dough making and mise en place areas organised.

Pizza Server

Sharing pizza you make with friends and family is the best. A pizza server is a good place to rest the pizza after taking it out of the oven. It's easy to pick up and perfect for getting food into people's hands.

How to Throw a Pizza Party

Pizza brings people together, or as we like to say, pizza is better together. Here's some quick guidance on how to set up so you're ready to host an epic pizza party.

Be prepared – buy ingredients and prep as much as you can ahead of the day.

Give yourself at least 24 hours to make dough before the party kicks off.

Ball your dough at least 6 hours before you want to start creating pizza, so they have time to relax and finish proofing.

Rule of thumb: make enough dough balls for a pizza per person. If you have leftover dough balls you can put them in the fridge to use the next day – don't be afraid to make extra dough balls; accidents happen and it's good to have a buffer.

Prep your work surface where you will open the dough and build pies. Make sure you have a clean and tidy area to work in, with everything in arm's reach. You're going to need the dough close to hand, a space to open the dough, a space to top the dough and to transfer the pizza to a peel, and a clean area for the pizza to be served and sliced. We recommend prepping a surface large enough to make 2 pizzas at a time.

Get your toppings arranged, organised and placed within easy reach of your workspace.

Buy ingredients to cater for everyone – vegan / vegetarian / meaty. Are your guests into the classics or ready to try something new?

Get the oven going early. The longer the oven heats up, the more saturated with heat the stone floor will become, and the more heat the floor will hold, so you have no delay between pizzas.

When your pizza comes out of the oven, have a dedicated surface where you can easily slice and then serve. A pizza server is a great tool to serve from so you can get the pizza going around to everyone.

Get friends involved and making their own pizza. This isn't a barbecue, everyone can get stuck in. If there are kids, get them involved too; they love to top their own pizzas and be part of the action.

Make some time to enjoy yourself too!

We recommend serving pizzas as they come out of the oven. The more people you get involved in making pizzas, the better the flow and energy of the party. If you insist on serving all your pizzas at once, you can par-bake them in advance, then flash bake them when your guests arrive, but there isn't anything better than eating fresh pizza the moment it's ready.

02 Ingredients

Tomatoes

Tomatoes are one of the cornerstone ingredients of pizza. Classic tomato sauce paired with a great crust and topped with cheese. Tomato goes beyond the classic sauce into toppings and sides. This is a quick guide to the right, fresh tomato for the job. Like anything, better-quality ingredients result in better pizza.

Cherry

Great for slow roasting – see our Roasted Tomato Sauce (page 87) or Confit Tomatoes (page 104). Generally these are much sweeter than larger tomatoes, with a good balance of tartness. Look for cherry tomatoes that are firm and smooth skinned.

Heirloom

An assortment of all shapes and sizes and colours. Great for salads and, most importantly, Caprese Pizza (page 132). Heirloom, or heritage, are varietals of tomatoes whose seeds are generationally passed down, and the fruit are highly regarded for their robust taste and juiciness.

Plum / Roma

Plum / Roma tomatoes make for great sauce, like Simple Tomato Sauce (page 82) or Marinara Tomato Sauce (page 84). Plum tomatoes vary slightly in size, taste and texture, but the essence of why they're great for pizza is the same: the elongated plum shape has more tomato flesh and fewer seeds, and the flesh is generally sweeter and has a lower water content than other varietals, making it great for breaking down into sauce. Italian San Marzano DOP are the most renowned – they go through rigorous quality control so they are a natural go-to – but they're not the only type we recommend.

Hand Crushed

Milled

Hand Blended

Herbs & Garnishes

Basil

The classic pizza herb. Keep the leaves whole, tear fresh leaves over a pizza, or use scissors to roughly chop a bunch to release the oils and maximise their fragrance. Basil can be used pre- or post-bake.

Oregano

Use fresh leaves or dried. The dried variety is milder in flavour, while the fresh is sharper and more peppery. Dried has a long shelf life and is a great garnish for pizza pre- or post-bake. A little oregano goes a long way, use sparingly.

Traditionally, herbs like basil and oregano are used on pizza, but it's fun to also experiment with other herbs and garnishes such as rosemary, thyme, flat-leaf parsley and mint to create your own distinct flavour combinations. Use herbs and garnishes to add complexity and craft to the pizza you create.

Rosemary

Great with so many things, especially for pizzas with chicken, mushrooms or potatoes (see our Roman Potato Pizza on page 166).

Thyme

This leafy herb has a strong scent and a sweet and nutty flavour, and works well on a white pizza and with cheeses such as ricotta.

Mint

Pairs well with roasted cherry tomatoes and tangy cheeses such as goat's cheese or halloumi, or even dessert pizzas.

Meats

The sky's the limit with meat on pizza. Take the purist's route and go with traditional Italian-origin cured meats such as prosciutto or the American-origin, global-favourite pepperoni. Alternatively, go wild and opt for ground beef, chicken or smoked bacon. Meat often adds more fat and salt to the pizza to fully explore your palate.

Cured meats

Great when added pre-bake to crisp and char in the oven or post-bake to retain texture and melt into a fresh and hot pizza. You can't go wrong with the Italian classics, such as salami, prosciutto, mortadella, soppressata and capicola (coppa). They contain the right amount of fat, and fat equals flavour.

The most popular topping has to be pepperoni, made from a mixture of pork and beef. Look for high-quality pepperoni that will curl and cup when baked on a pizza.

Less traditional

You can also try adding fresh bacon, Italian sausage, meatballs, ground beef or chicken for a unique flavour combination. Just remember to pre-cook these meats before adding them to your pizza.

Vegetables

Get creative with veg on pizza. Depending on the bake time, most vegetables such as peppers, potatoes, mushrooms, onions, broccoli and chard benefit from being pre-cooked before baking the pizza. This pre-cooking removes some of the water content from the veg and stops the pizza from being soggy. Try the Pizza Bianca (page 119).

Cheese

Cheese melts, combining fat with the acid and sugars from the tomato and crust of the dough, to help pizza become the perfect food that it is.

Mozzarella

Fresh Italian mozzarella – this has a high moisture content and is a traditional Neapolitan pizza staple. The high water content can mean there's a risk of the cheese settling as a puddle and resulting in soggy pizza, so be sure to dry off as much excess water as possible. With the high heat from a pizza oven you'll get it melting into pools of stretchy, creamy delight.

Buffalo mozzarella – made from buffalo milk. If you're a purist, mozzarella di bufala from Campania, Italy, is the best choice, made according to regulated production rules defined by Consorzio di Tutela. There are other buffalo mozzarella options out there, all with a higher fat content that combines nicely with the savory dough and sweet, acidic sauce.

Fior di latte – made from cow's milk in the same style as Italian mozzarella. A mild and creamy fresh mozzarella that melts well.

Low-moisture aged mozzarella – as the name suggests, this mozzarella has less water content. There's less risk of soupy pizza with this cheese, and it's great for cheese pulls. The lower moisture has better browning and stretching abilities when cooked in a pizza oven, creating a great texture and rich flavour. We would always recommend buying a whole brick of mozzarella rather than pre-shredded cheese. This cheese can be found used on the classic New York Plain Cheese Pizza (page 140) and many other styles of pizza in the recipe section. It never forgets to stretch.

Hard cheeses

Grate or shave onto a freshly baked pizza for that finishing touch.

Parmigiano Reggiano – made from cow's milk, this cheese has a nutty super umami flavour profile and is amazing with tomatoes. The original when it comes to finishing the perfect pizza. Use pre- and post-bake to garnish.

Pecorino Romano – made from sheep's milk. Saltier, with a stronger, sharper taste than Parmigiano. Can be used in the same way as Parm – some prefer its flavour. As with most things, go with your personal preference. Both cheeses are lactose free.

Soft cheeses

Great for dolloping onto your pizza pre- or post-bake. A burrata with pepperoni and hot honey is a favourite. Ricotta mixed with pepper on a Cacio e Pepe Pizza (page 162) is mind blowing.

Tips	Other cheeses to try: provolone, cheddar, taleggio.

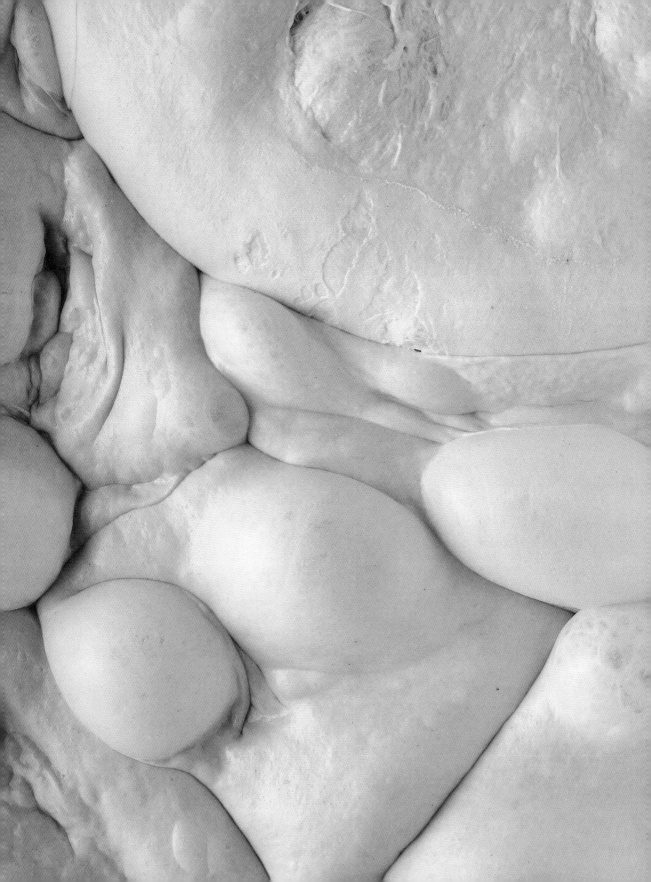

03 Dough

Understanding Dough

Baker's Percentage

Baker's Percentage or Baker's Math is a simple way of proportioning an ingredient relative to the amount of flour, with flour being 100%. The amount of flour is always 100%. Example: 1000g (35.3oz) of flour and 680g (24oz) of water = 68%. All ingredients for the dough will be measured by weight as a percentage of flour weight. Different dough recipes rely on the right percentage of flour to water. This is a really easy way to scale up or down recipes or batches.

Hydration

Hydration or Hydration Rate is simply the amount of water in dough. What makes one pizza dough different than the next is largely based on the proportion of water to flour. This is expressed as a percentage of water relative to the amount of flour (see Baker's Percentage). This enables you to always repeat a recipe accurately despite the batch size or recipe. Too much water or too little water will affect the texture of the dough, making it stiff or sticky.

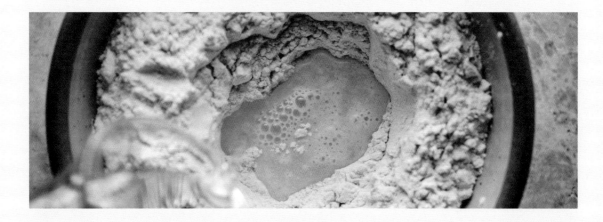

Fermentation

Fermentation refers to the process by which microorganisms such as yeast, bacteria and other natural enzymes break down the carbohydrates in the dough to produce carbon dioxide gas. This gas causes the dough to rise and gives bread its characteristic texture and flavour. During fermentation, the dough is allowed to rest at room temperature or in the fridge from several hours to a couple of days. This allows the microorganisms to work their magic. See pages 74–77 for further information.

Proofing

After balling the dough, proofing is the dough's final rise. Carbon dioxide causes the dough to expand and become lighter and fluffier. Over-proofing, or allowing the dough to rise too much, can result in a flat or misshapen final product, while under-proofing can result in pizza with a tough, chewy texture. Proper proofing is crucial to achieving great pizza.

Flour, Yeast & Salt

The more you learn about pizza, the more you will realise what a difference the dough makes, and which ingredients make a really good dough. When you break it down, pizza dough is beautiful in its simplicity. Three ingredients mixed with water: flour, yeast and salt.

Types of Flour

There are three types of flour we recommend for making great pizza dough: '00', plain and bread flour. Flour types can be categorised by different textures and protein content. Protein content translates to the amount of gluten. Which flour you choose to use will affect your dough's crust in terms of crispness, open and airy hole structure, and chew. Certain types of flour create a crispier crust, while others give you a chewier crust.

Gluten is the natural protein network that remains when starch is removed from wheat, and it is what gives pizza dough its stretchy consistency and, when fired, its texture. When flour is mixed with water it creates an elastic structure throughout the dough, giving pizza its fantastic chew. The more gluten in the flour, the chewier the crust will be.

Different pizza styles require different amounts of protein. Pizza flours range from 9–15% protein content. High protein can mean a firmer and stronger dough; lower-protein flour will produce a softer dough. Different flours absorb different amounts of water, with higher protein being able to take on more for those high-hydration dough recipes.

'00' Flour

For Neapolitan purists, '00' – or Tipo 00 – is ideal for pizza dough for two reasons: it is finely ground and has a lower gluten (protein) level than most flours. The '00' refers to the texture and fineness of the flour. Italians classify their flour by numbers according to how finely they are ground, '00' is the finest. It typically has a 12% protein content. '00' flour produces a traditional crust that is thin and airy, perfect for Neapolitan-style pizza. This means that '00' flour will produce a pizza dough that's stronger than a pizza dough made with plain (all-purpose) flour due to its higher gluten content but it will be less strong than dough made with bread flour due to the wheat variety.

Plain (all-purpose) Flour

Not just a clever name, plain (all-purpose) flour does a good job for a lot of purposes, including pizza. It has a protein content of 9–11%. Due to its lower gluten content than other flours, the dough won't rise as high as a dough that contains more protein. It will taste good in most pizza dough recipes and is readily available, however it can sometimes be more difficult to stretch as it may tear easily.

Bread Flour

Bread flour has a higher amount of protein than plain (all-purpose) flour, about 12–15%. Bread flour results in a stretchy dough that's less likely to tear, with a thick, soft and fluffy crust. It's great for pan pizza and works well for thick crusts. Bread flour will make a pizza that's crispy without the soft pillowy crusts you see when you use '00' flour. You get a chewier, more bread-like pizza crust when you make your dough with bread flour. The key is to bring the dough to room temperature and give it a decent rest before stretching. As mentioned, bread flour won't easily tear as you stretch it out.

Semolina

Semolina flour is made from durum wheat, which is different to the soft wheat used in other flours. This type of flour has a high gluten content, but the gluten acts differently. What makes semolina so great in pizza making is its ability to prevent sticking: use it when opening your dough balls, on your work surface and on the placement peel. Semolina has a larger particle size, and these act like ball bearings to make it easier to slide the uncooked pizza into the oven. We recommend you use fine semolina like rimacinata when opening up dough balls and launching pizzas.

Yeast

Yeast is the 'living' part of the dough. It feeds on the sugar in the dough and releases carbon dioxide as a by-product. This is what the tiny bubbles as the dough rises are, stretching out the gluten network present in the dough, giving your pizza its texture.

Fresh yeast: also known as cake or beer yeast, comes in a compressed form and needs to be refrigerated. It typically isn't that readily available, but many think it tastes better. You also don't need to use small portions when using fresh yeast either, so it's a little easier to measure out. However, it does have a short shelf life.

Active dry yeast: yeast that has had about 90% of its moisture content removed, and comes in packets. Easy to find and has a long shelf life.

Follow the instructions on the packet – some yeasts are fast-acting and therefore will proof your dough much quicker than others. Some may require activating with warm water.

Salt

Salt affects the flavour of your dough; it affects the structure too. It influences the fermentation process, slowing it down. Salt strengthens the gluten strands, making the dough stronger and enabling carbon dioxide bubbles to be held within the dough. So, don't forget the salt.

It is important to accurately weigh your salt: use baker's percentage (page 38) even when adding salt.

When choosing salt, avoid iodised table salt and instead opt for flaky sea salt, Kosher, or the least refined option you know.

How to
Mix Dough by Hand

The primary difference between hand-mixing dough and machine-mixing dough is the level of control over the mixing process and the amount of physical effort required.

Hand-mixing dough involves combining the ingredients by hand, usually in a mixing bowl. The dough is kneaded by hand to develop the gluten and create a smooth, elastic texture. Hand mixing allows the user to feel the texture of the dough as they go and adjust the mixing process accordingly. However, hand mixing can be time consuming and physically demanding, especially for large batches of dough.

1. Using digital scales, start by measuring out the ingredients as stated in your chosen dough recipe. To weigh the yeast, it's best to use digital scales that can weigh less than a gram for accuracy.

2. Add the water to a large mixing bowl, then add the yeast and optional preferment (poolish, see page 74), and stir to dissolve.

3. Add the flour to the bowl and, with a dough scraper, make a circular motion around the bowl to combine all of the ingredients until they form a mass and there are no dry bits of flour left. During this process, let the scraper do all the hard work and try and keep your hands as clean as possible for as long as you can. Take your time during this process (it will take about 5 minutes).

4. Once the dough has formed a single mass, use the dough scraper to transfer it to the clean counter. With your non-dominant hand holding down the part of the dough nearest to you, grab the side of the dough with your dominant hand and stretch it out away from you. Fold the dough back on itself, then reset by grabbing the side of the dough with your dominant hand and holding the dough down with your other hand. Repeat the stretch. Continue this motion for 5 minutes. Add the salt and continue this motion for a further 3–5 minutes until all the salt has dissolved into the dough and the dough has become smooth, indicating that the gluten has developed.

5. You can use the 'windowpane' test to check the gluten strength of your dough by stretching the dough with your fingers to see if you can see light through it without the dough tearing.

6. Use the dough scraper to remove any dough that has stuck to your hands to add it back into the main dough.

7. Follow the bulk fermentation instructions of your chosen dough recipe.

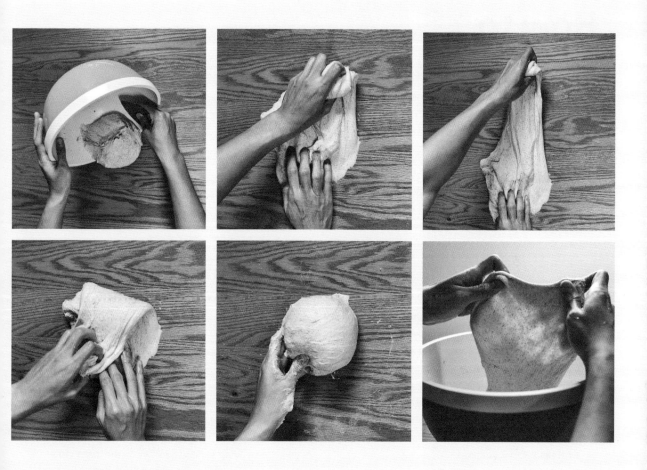

Use a bowl when mixing high-hydration dough

How to
Mix Dough by Machine

The two main types of machines available for a home baker: a planetary/stand mixer or a spiral mixer. Spiral mixers are more suitable for making bread and pizza dough, as they achieve a better mix and keep the dough cooler for longer. Planetary mixers are a multi-function kitchen workhorse, which often come with a dough hook attachment.

The key benefits of using a machine are that they are more practical for mixing very high hydration doughs and involve less effort for bigger batches than mixing by hand.

1. Using digital scales, start by measuring out the ingredients as stated in your chosen dough recipe. To weigh the yeast, it's best to use digital scales that can weigh less than a gram for accuracy. When using a machine, you can achieve great results by dividing the water into 2 batches:
    First water: used to combine the ingredients during the first part of the mix – takes the dough to around 60% hydration.
    Second water: used to bassinage – a French baking term for adding water slowly later in the mix. This method allows you to add more water to your dough, rather than if you just add it all at once. This helps achieve a nice crumb structure.

2. Add the first water, yeast and optional preferment to the bowl and mix on low speed until the yeast has dissolved. Add all the flour and mix on low speed (5–10 minutes) until there is no dry flour left. Scrape the bowl with a dough scraper if needed to ensure all the flour is incorporated.

3. Add the second water little by little. When you have just 10–20g (0.7oz) of water left, turn the mixer to medium speed, add the salt and continue adding the water until there is none left over, and the salt has combined.

4. Stop the mixer and rest the dough for a minute or so.

5. If there is oil in the recipe, restart the mixer on medium speed and slowly add the oil until it's all combined.

6. Next, stop the mixer and rest the dough for about 5 minutes before removing the dough and finishing it on the clean counter by gently pulling it towards you and building surface tension on the dough to create a large smooth doughball ready for bulk fermentation.

7. Follow the bulk fermentation instructions of your chosen dough recipe.

Tips

For consistent results, it's good practice to measure the temperature of your dough before, during and after the mixing process to make sure it doesn't get too warm. Warmer dough will proof faster than colder dough. An ideal temperature to finish your dough mixing is 23°C/73°F. During the warmer months, your dough temperature can be managed during the mixing process by using ice-cold water.

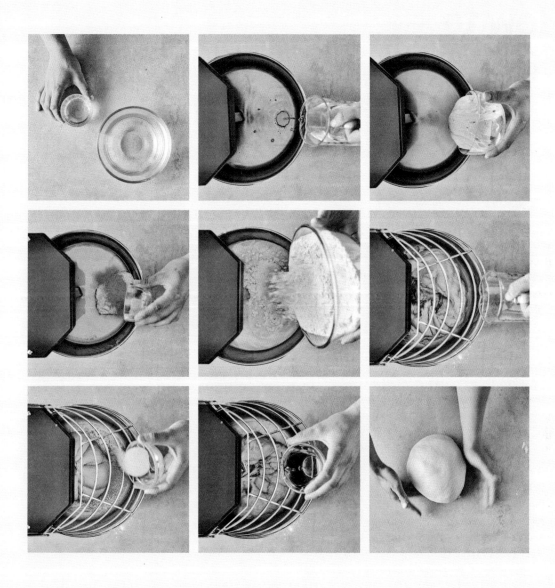

How to Ball Dough

Proper balling of dough gives the dough its form and shape that later allows you to open up the dough into that beautiful round classic pizza shape.

To ball up dough, follow these steps.

1. With a dough cutter, divide and weigh the dough into pieces. If the dough is sticky and wet at this stage, working fast is key.
2. Once the dough has been divided, ball the dough by folding it in and under itself. This builds surface tension on the top of the ball and makes it smooth out into a round.
3. Sit the dough balls back down on the counter to rest for 2 minutes. Be careful not to leave them for too long or the dough will start to form a skin. You do not need to add any flour at this stage.
4. Flip the ball over in your hand and pinch the dough together to seal it. This ensures that you won't get any thin spots when opening and stretching your dough later.
5. Place the balls in a dough tray or bowl. Make sure each ball is spaced around two-fingers-width apart from each other to allow room for them to expand as they proof. Time will vary dependant on recipe.

How to Stretch Dough

This method is applicable for round pizza bases, such as New York-style dough and Neapolitan-style dough. By stretching your pizza dough ball, you will create a uniform shape and thickness that will help ensure even baking and delicious pizza. Remember to handle the dough gently.

Before stretching, ensure you have given your dough balls a minimum of 3 hours to proof at room temperature. Time will vary depending on your recipe and the ambient temperature of the room.

An ideal temperature for stretching dough is 19–20°C (66–68°F). If the dough balls get too warm, they can become harder to manage by tearing and sticking to the peel more easily. Once removed from the fridge, the dough balls will begin their final proof and will grow as they fill with air. If the dough balls become too full of air, they will start to become hard to manage, so you want to let the balls get to a size just before they start to get out of hand. If you see big bubbles forming on the surface of the balls, then they could have gone too far: the dough is still usable and will make great-tasting pizza but can be harder to manage.

A properly mixed, relaxed and proofed dough should feel very easy to open. A good dough has the right balance of elasticity and extensibility: elasticity is the dough's opposition to stretching and extensibility is the dough's ability to stretch.

1. Once your dough has proofed, remove it from the tray. Using semolina here helps to act as a barrier to stop the dough sticking to your hand or the cutter.

2. Place your dough ball in a bowl of semolina flour, flip it over and cover both sides, making sure the whole dough ball is coated. This ensures that there are no sticky bits on the dough ball that will complicate the stretching. After this, your dough ball should be free and easy to move around on the counter.

3. Make sure it is as round as possible before you start pushing the air to the crust. If a dough ball doesn't start round, then you won't end up with a round pizza. Push the air to the crusts from the centre outwards, flip it over and repeat. You're aiming to open the base to the size of your hand with an even perimeter of around 2.5cm (1in).

4. Once the dough ball is opened you can stretch it in several ways. A great method for beginners is to transfer the base to the backs of your hands, making sure to support most of the weight of the dough. Gently turn the base while using gravity to let it slowly stretch. The traditional Neapolitan slap-style involves keeping one hand on the base while using the other to gently stretch the base and give it a 90-degree turn. This allows greater speed and precision but is also a method that requires some practice.

5. Once your dough has stretched, shake off any excess semolina, place it down on a lightly floured surface and it's ready to top.

Dough Problems & Solutions

Whether you are a beginner or pro, when working with dough, mistakes happen. Sure, the better you get the fewer mistakes you make, but even then, if you do make a mistake, it's knowing how to quickly fix it so that you can move on. It's all part of the pizza journey. Here are a few tips and tricks to help you get back on track when things go a little awry.

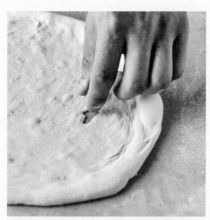

Hole in Dough

Over-stretched dough can result in holes. It happens to the best of us. Don't quit the pizza, simply pinch them back together again.

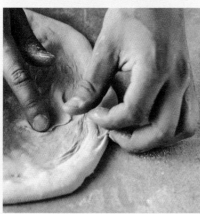

Over-proofed Dough

Over-proofing can happen when the dough gets too warm or too much yeast was used in the making. Over-proofing causes the dough to be hard to work with, and when handled, the dough ball can deflate. The dough will never reach its pinnacle, but all is not lost – you can still make pizza. There are 2 options: 1) re-ball the dough and set it back in the fridge, overnight ideally but even a few hours will at least improve the over-proofing. 2) use the dough for a calzone (see page 184).

Under-proofed Dough

When it's cold – or you haven't allowed enough time for the proofing process – your dough will have a bad time. Pizza dough wants to be warm (but not too warm), and it needs time to sit comfortably and do its thing. For a long while. If you rush this process, chances are your dough will not have had enough time to proof. Under-proofed dough is lifeless. It will not be full of air and will be tough to open. The good news is that all under-proofed dough needs is time, and a room-temperature climate will get it to where it needs to be. If that's not an option, you can speed the process up a little bit by putting the dough in a warm spot. If neither of these tactics do the trick, then it's likely the yeast that you used is dead.

Sticky Dough / Sticking to Peel

Can't get the pizza on the peel? Can't get the pizza off the peel? When you're starting out 'failure to launch' can be a common problem, but there's an easy solution. Flour. Add flour to your work surface before opening your dough ball. Sprinkle flour on your peel before placing your pizza on it. The flour will help the dough move from surface to surface. Some people like to use the same flour they made their dough with, some people like to use semolina flour (which acts like tiny baker's ball bearings). Another tip is to add your sauce and toppings to your pizza before you put it on the peel. The less time the pizza is on the peel, the less likely it is to stick! Keep it short and sweet.

How to
Top, Place & Turn

Top

This is the act of putting your toppings on your open dough base. When topping your pizza, less is more. Be careful not to overload the base with toppings as it can weigh the pizza down and make it harder to get off the peel.

You can either top your pizza on a peel, or off (and transfer it to the peel once it's topped). In either case, you should make sure the peel is clean, dry and has been lightly dusted with flour before the pizza goes on to make sure the base does not stick. Once the pizza goes onto the peel, the clock is ticking – the longer the pizza is sat on the peel the more chance there is of it sticking.

Once topped, if transferring to the peel, lift one edge of the pizza and confidently push the peel under the pizza from a low 10-degree angle. Then, gently stretch out the pizza to the edges of the peel to finesse the circular shape and redistribute the toppings if required, to ensure everything is in the right place. Shake the peel to remove any excess flour, if there's too much this can burn and make the crust taste bitter.

Remember, when topping your pizza, less is more.

Place

Launch the pizza into the oven by placing the peel halfway into the oven and then shimmy the pizza off the peel with a few movements. Try not to sit the pizza too close to the flame. Imagine you are trying to pull a tablecloth from under a plate without the plate flying off the table! Once you gain more experience, you'll be able to do this in one confident movement; practice is key.

Turn

Keep an eye on your pizza while it's in the oven. Once the base has begun to set, after 30–40 seconds, use a turning peel to spin the pizza 180 degrees, then continue to turn the pizza 90 degrees every 10 seconds thereafter, making sure to try and keep the pizza in the same spot in the oven, until the pizza bakes to the colour you like. Pull the pizza out onto a board or pizza server, slice and enjoy!

Tips	Move your pizza from the oven onto a wire baking rack until you're ready to slice and serve to avoid soggy pizza.

| Tips | Failure to launch? Pizza keep sticking to the peel? Use flour on the peel to prevent sticking. | Remember to use the turning peel to rotate the pizza and ensure a consistent bake. |

How to
Make Pan Pizza

Detroit, Sicilian, Grandma, Focaccia, Pizza al Taglia... there are many types and styles of pan pizza and each will have a different recipe, but they all share similarities – rectangular or square pizza, baked in a pan, with a thick crust that is crispy on the bottom and edges, but soft and airy on the inside. The pizza dough is typically made with bread flour for its high-protein properties, either 100% or mixed with another flour, and is baked in an oiled pan, which gives it its characteristic crispy and caramelised crust. Due to the square or rectangular nature of pan pizzas, it's no surprise that they are cut and served as a square. They are sturdy, easy to hold and even better to eat!

For pan pizzas, we recommend par-baking the dough before topping them, as without the weight of the toppings it allows the dough to properly rise, or spring, making for an open, light and airy crust. For Detroit-style pizza the sauce is often placed on top of the cheese – some people do this pre-bake, but we like to warm the sauce separately and ladle it on after the pizza comes out the oven; not only does it look cool but it helps to prevent the crust from becoming soggy. Overall, pan pizza is known for its thick, crunchy crust, tangy tomato sauce and generous cheese and toppings.

1. Using a pan or tray of your choice – we recommend either a square 25.4cm (10in) or rectangular 25.5 x 20cm (10 x 8in) pan – add a little olive or canola oil and evenly spread it around the pan with your hand.

2. Take a cold fermented dough ball directly from the fridge and place it in the pan, oil your fingers and dimple the dough, pushing it to the corners of the pan, then cover and leave at room temperature. Repeat this method 4–5 times at 20-minute intervals. As soon as the dough has reached and filled all four corners of the pan, cover and allow to proof at room temperature until the dough has doubled in volume and looks puffy and full of air (this time can vary).

3. With generously oiled fingertips, dimple the dough again. Place the pan in the oven, turn the flame off and place a door over the oven opening. Par-bake for 2 minutes, then rotate 180 degrees, replace the door and bake for another 2 minutes. Remove and allow the dough to rest at room temperature. Turn the oven flame back on and preheat to 330°C (625°F) (stone floor temperature).

4. Top the pizza. Turn the flame off, then gently launch the pan back into the oven and bake for 4 minutes with the door on. Rotate the pizza 180 degrees after 2 minutes.

5. After about 4 minutes, remove the door and turn the flame up to high to obtain a bit more colour while rotating the pizza frequently for another couple of minutes depending on how you like the crust.

6. Once baked, remove from the pan immediately with an offset spatula. Place onto a cooling screen or wire rack and rest for about 1 minute before garnishing and slicing as per your chosen recipe.

Signature-style Pizza Dough

This is where we recommend you start your journey of making your own pizza dough at home. The recipe has been tested in the Gozney kitchen and proven in countless households across the world. It is designed to be on the forgiving side for pizza beginners and chefs alike, and the results will be epic.

Prep Time
1 hour

Proof Time
24-48 hours

Makes
4 x 350g (12.3oz) dough balls for 14-inch pizzas
Or 6 x 250g (8.8oz) dough balls for 12-inch pizzas

Plain or bread flour 1000g / 35.2g / 100%
Cold water 600g / 21.8oz / 60%
Dry yeast 2g / 0.07oz / 0.2%
Salt 25g / 0.9oz / 2.5%
Olive oil 25g / 0.9oz / 2.5%

1. Divide the water into two batches: 590g (20.8oz) (first water) and 10g (0.3oz) (second water).
2. Add the first water and yeast to the mixer and mix on slow speed for a couple of minutes until the yeast has dissolved.
3. Add the flour to the mixer and mix on slow speed for 5 minutes until all the flour has combined and there are no dry bits left.
4. Stop the mixer and rest the dough for 1–2 minutes.
5. Add the salt along with the second water and mix on medium speed for a further 2 minutes until all the salt has been combined.
6. Allow the mix to rest for a few minutes before turning the mixer back on to medium speed while slowly adding in the olive oil.
7. Allow the dough to rest for 5 minutes before removing it from the mixer.
8. Divide and shape the dough into 350g (12.3oz) balls for a 14-inch pizza or 250g (8.8oz) for a 12-inch pizza and place into a dough tray with a lid. Leave at room temperature for 1 hour, then place in the fridge to ferment for 24–48 hours.
9. After removing from the fridge, let the dough balls sit at room temperature for 3–6 hours before baking (time will vary based on the room temperature).
10. Alternatively, the dough balls can be proofed at room temperature for 8–10 hours and baked the same day.

Tips

You may need to periodically stop the mixer and scrape down the bowl to ensure all the flour is mixed in.

Neapolitan-style Pizza Dough

Neapolitan-style pizza originated from the streets of Napoli. It's loved for its puffy crusts and soft structure. Traditionally it's a 24-hour ferment made up of only a few simple ingredients – flour, water, salt and yeast.

Prep Time
1 hour

Proof Time
24–48 hours

Makes
6 x 260g (9.2oz) dough balls for 11–12-inch pizzas

'00' flour 1000g / 35oz / 100%
Cold water 600g / 21oz / 60%
Dry yeast 2g / 0.07oz / 0.2%
Salt 30g / 0.88oz / 3%

1. Divide the water into two batches: 590–595g (20.8–21oz) (first water) and 5–10g (0.2–0.3oz) (second water).
2. Add the first water and yeast to the mixer and mix on slow speed for a couple of minutes until the yeast has dissolved.
3. Add the flour to the mixer and mix on slow speed until all the flour has combined and there are no dry bits left.
4. Stop the mixer and rest the dough for 1–2 minutes.
5. Add the salt along with the second water and mix on medium speed for a further 2 minutes until all the salt has been combined.
6. Allow the dough to rest for 5 minutes before removing it from the mixer. If you wish to freeze any dough, after removing it from the mixer, divide it into desired portions and freeze it before it begins fermenting.
7. Form the dough into a big ball. Place in a bowl, cover and leave at room temperature for 3–4 hours.
8. Divide and shape the dough into 260g (9.2oz) dough balls, transfer to a dough tray and cover. Leave at room temperature for 30 minutes to 1 hour, then place in the fridge to ferment for 24–48 hours.
9. After removing from the fridge, let the dough balls sit at room temperature for 3–6 hours before baking (time will vary based on the room temperature).

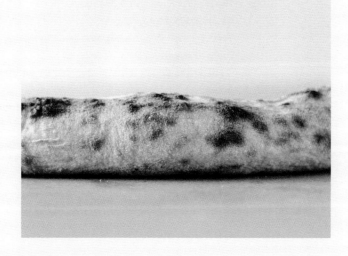

Tom's 96-Hour Pizza Dough

On Tom Gozney's own pizza journey, he's spent hours in the kitchen experimenting with dough; it became an obsession and a weekly ritual. This 96-hour dough recipe is Tom's signature.

Prep Time
1 hour

Proof Time
96 hours

Makes
6 x 270g (9.5oz) dough balls for 12-inch pizzas

'00' flour or bread flour 1000g / 35oz / 100%
Cold water 650g / 22.9oz / 65%
Dry yeast 1.5g / 0.05oz / 0.15%
Salt 25g / 0.88oz / 2.5%

1. Divide the water into two batches: 600g (21.2oz) (first water) and 50g (1.8oz) (second water).
2. Add the first water and yeast to the mixer and mix on slow speed for a couple of minutes to combine until the yeast has dissolved.
3. Add the flour to the mixer and mix on slow speed for 5 minutes until all the flour has combined and there are no dry bits left.
4. Stop the mixer and rest the dough for 1–2 minutes.
5. Restart the mixer on slow speed and slowly pour in the second water, in small amounts, waiting for each amount to combine before adding the next (this will take around 5 minutes).
6. With the last remaining 10–20g (0.35–0.7oz) of water, add the salt and mix on medium speed for a further 2 minutes until all the salt has been combined.
7. Allow the dough to rest for 5 minutes before removing it from the mixer. If you wish to freeze any dough, after removing it from the mixer, divide it into desired portions and freeze it before it begins fermenting.
8. Form the dough into a big ball. Place in a bowl, cover and leave at room temperature for 4 hours.
9. Transfer the dough to the fridge to bulk ferment for 48 hours as one mass.
10. After 48 hours, remove the dough from the fridge and leave at room temperature for 1 hour. Divide and shape into 270g (9.5oz) balls, place into a dough tray and cover. Leave at room temperature for 1 hour, then transfer to the fridge for a further 48 hours.
11. After removing from the fridge, let the dough balls sit at room temperature for 3–6 hours before baking (time will vary based on the room temperature).

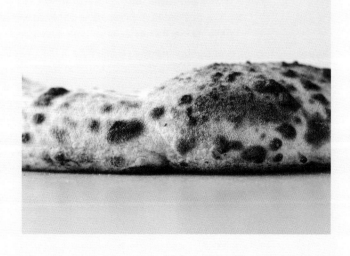

New York-style Pizza Dough

Better than a dollar slice. From Brooklyn to Manhattan and beyond, New York has left its stamp on the pizza world. Here's our version of a great New York-style dough you can do at home.

Prep Time
1 hour

_____

Main Dough

Bread flour 1000g / 35oz / 93%
Cold water 590g / 2oz / 59%
Poolish 150g / 5.3oz / 15%
   (page 74)
Dry yeast 2g / 0.07oz / 0.18%
Salt 25g / 0.88oz / 2.3%
Olive oil 40g / 1.5oz / 3.7%

Totals (including poolish)

Flour 1075g / 38oz / 100%
Water 665g / 23.4oz / 61.8%

Proof Time
24–48 hours

Makes
4 x 350g (12.3oz) dough balls for 14-inch pizzas Or 7 x 250g (8.8oz) dough balls for 12-inch pizzas

1. Divide the water into two batches: 570g (20.1oz) (first water) and 20g (0.7oz) (second water).
2. Add the first water, yeast and poolish to the mixer and mix on slow speed for a couple of minutes to combine.
3. Add the flour to the mixer and mix on slow speed for 5 minutes until all the flour has combined and there are no dry bits left.
4. Stop the mixer and rest the dough for 1–2 minutes.
5. Add the salt along with the second water and mix on medium speed for a further 2 minutes until all the salt has been combined.
6. Stop the mixer and let the dough rest for 2 minutes.
7. Restart the mixer on medium speed and add the oil gradually until it's all combined.
8. Allow the dough to rest for 5 minutes before removing it from the mixer. If you wish to freeze any dough, after removing it from the mixer, divide it into desired portions and freeze it before it begins fermenting.
9. Divide and shape the dough into 350g (12.3oz) balls for a 14-inch pizza or 250g (8.8oz) for a 12-inch pizza and place into a dough tray. Cover with a lid and leave at room temperature for 1–2 hours, then place in the fridge to ferment for 24–48 hours.
10. After removing from the fridge, let the dough balls sit at room temperature for 3–6 hours before baking (time will vary based on the room temperature).
11. Alternatively, the dough balls can be proofed at room temperature for 8–10 hours and baked the same day.

Sourdough Pizza Dough

Sourdough pizza dough is extremely versatile and a great all-rounder, but it is a labour of love. It takes a little longer to ferment and proof. The addition of the sourdough preferment (page 78) gives this dough amazing flavour and signature airy texture. It's a little more fragile than other pizza doughs so needs to be handled with extra care.

Prep Time
1 hour

Proof Time
24–72 hours

Makes
6 x 270g (9.5oz) dough balls for 12-inch pizzas

Main Dough
'00' flour 660g / 14oz / 64%
Bread flour 340g / 7.4oz / 33%
Cold water 693g / 24oz / 67%
Starter 50g / 1oz / 5% (page 78)
Salt 31g / 0.6oz / 3%

Totals (including starter)
Flour 1025g / 35oz / 100%
Water 718g / 25oz / 70%

1. Divide the water into two batches: 590g (20.8oz) (first water) and 103g (3.6oz) (second water).
2. Add the first water and the starter to the mixer and mix on a slow speed for a couple of minutes to combine.
3. Add both flours to the mixer and mix on slow speed for 5 minutes until all the flour has combined and there are no dry bits left.
4. Stop the mixer and rest the dough for 2 minutes.
5. Restart the mixer on slow speed and slowly pour in the second water, in small amounts, waiting for each amount to combine before adding the next (this will take about 5 minutes).
6. With the remaining 10–20g (0.35–0.7oz) water, add the salt and mix on medium speed for a further 2 minutes until all the salt has been combined.
7. Stop the mixer and allow the dough to rest for 5 minutes before removing it from the mixer.
8. Form the dough into a big ball, place into a bowl, cover and leave at room temperature for 5–6 hours before transferring to the fridge for 24–72 hours.
9. Remove the dough from the fridge. Divide and shape into 270g (9.5oz) balls, transfer to a dough tray and cover. Leave to sit at room temperature for 6–8 hours for the final proof or until the dough has doubled in size and is full of air (time will vary based on the room temperature).

Pan Pizza Dough
(Detroit-style and Sicilian-style)

Another great all-rounder is pan pizza like Detroit and Sicilian-style. This dough is typically made with bread flour to give you a super light and airy structure with crispy sides and base.

Prep Time
1 hour

Proof Time
24–48 hours

Makes
6 x 300g (10.5oz) dough ball for a 10 x 8-inch pan Or 4 x 450g (16oz) dough ball for a 10 x 10-inch pan

_____

Main Dough
Bread flour 900g / 35oz / 84%
Semolina rimacinata 100g / 3.5oz / 9%
Cold water 700g / 20oz / 65%
Poolish 150g / 5.3oz / 15%
   (page 74)
Dry yeast 2g / 0.07oz / 0.18%
Salt 25g / 0.88oz / 2.3%
Olive oil 50g / 1.7oz / 4.6%

Totals (including poolish)
Flour 1075g / 38oz / 100%
Water 775g / 27.3oz / 72%

1. Divide the water into two batches: 570g (20.1oz) (first water) and 130g (4.6oz) (second water).
2. Add the first water, the yeast and the poolish to the mixer and mix on slow speed for a couple of minutes to combine.
3. Add both flours to the mixer and mix on slow speed for 5 minutes until all the flour has combined and there are no dry bits left.
4. Stop the mixer and rest the dough for 2 minutes.
5. Restart the mixer on slow speed and slowly pour in the second water, in small amounts, waiting for each amount to combine before adding the next (about 5 minutes).
6. With the last remaining 10–20g (0.35–0.7oz) water, add the salt and mix on medium speed for a further 2 minutes until all the salt has been combined.
7. Stop the mixer and let the dough rest for 5 minutes.
8. Restart the mixer on medium speed and add the oil gradually until it's all combined.
9. Allow the dough to rest for 5 minutes before removing it from the mixer. If you wish to freeze any dough, after removing it from the mixer, divide it into desired portions and freeze it before it begins fermenting.
10. Form the dough into a big ball. Place in a bowl, cover and leave at room temperature for 1 hour.
11. Divide and shape the dough into your desired portion size. Transfer to a dough tray, cover and place into the fridge to ferment for 24–48 hours.
12. Once the dough has been removed from the fridge, it's ready to transfer to an oiled pizza pan – see page 54 on 'How to Make a Pan Pizza'.

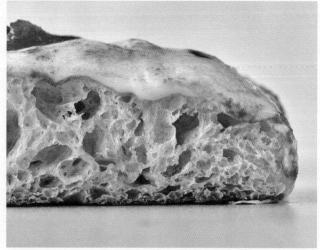

Roman-style Pizza Dough

Originating in Rome, this is a high-hydration dough that's light and crispy. The oil adds richness to the dough and gives a golden crust.

Prep Time
1 hour

Proof Time
24-48 hours

Makes
9 x 180g (6.3oz) dough balls for 12-inch pizzas

Bread flour 700g / 24.7oz / 30%
Semolina 300g / 10.6oz / 70%
Cold water 700g / 24.7oz / 70%
Dry yeast 2g / 0.07oz / 0.2%
Salt 30g / 1.2oz / 3%
Olive oil 50g / 1.8oz / 5%

1. Divide the water into two batches: 600g (21.2oz) (first water) and 100g (3.5oz) (second water).
2. Add the first water and yeast to the mixer and mix on a slow speed for a couple of minutes to combine until the yeast dissolves.
3. Add both flours to the mixer and mix on slow speed for 5 minutes until all the flour has combined and there are no dry bits left.
4. Stop the mixer and rest the dough for 1–2 minutes.
5. Restart the mixer on slow speed and slowly pour in the second water, in small amounts, waiting for each amount to combine before adding the next (this will take about 5 minutes).
6. With the last remaining 10–20g (0.35–0.7oz) water, add the salt and mix on medium speed for a further 2 minutes until all the salt has been combined.
7. Allow the dough to rest for 5 minutes before removing from the mixer. If you wish to freeze any dough, after removing it from the mixer, divide it into desired portions and freeze it before it begins fermenting.
8. Form the dough into a big ball. Place in a bowl, cover and leave at room temperature for 1–2 hours.
9. Divide and shape the dough into 180g (6.3oz) balls and place into a dough tray with a lid. Leave at room temperature for 1 hour, then place in the fridge for 24–48 hours.
10. Once the dough balls have been removed from the fridge, let them sit at room temperature for at least 3 hours before baking (time will vary based on the room temperature).
11. Alternatively, the dough balls can be proofed at room temperature for 6–8 hours and baked the same day.

Focaccia Dough

Another Italian classic. This is a high-hydration dough, which is made with the biga preferment (page 76). The combination gives you a very light and airy crumb.

Prep Time
1 hour

Proof Time
12–24 hours

Makes
3 x 550g (19.4oz) dough balls for a 10 x 12-inch pan

Main Dough
Bread flour (high-gluten
   preferred) 250g / 8.8oz / 25%
Biga 1130g / 39.8oz (See below)
Cold water 375g / 13.2oz / 37.5%
Salt 30g / 1oz / 3%
Extra virgin olive oil
   70g / 2.4oz / 7%

Biga (see page 76)
High-protein bread flour
   750g / 26.4oz / 75%
Water 375g / 13.2oz / 37.5%
Dry yeast 4g / 0.14oz / 0.4%

Totals (including biga)
Flour 1000g / 35.2oz / 100%
Water 750g / 26.4oz / 75%

1. Divide the water into two batches: 225g (8oz) (first water) and 150g (5.3oz) (second water).
2. Break the biga into chunks and place them into the mixer. Add the first water and flour and mix on slow speed for a couple of minutes to combine.
3. Stop the mixer and rest the dough for 2 minutes.
4. Restart the mixer on slow speed and slowly pour in the second water, in small amounts, waiting for each amount to combine before adding the next (this will take about 5 minutes).
5. With the last remaining 10–20g (0.35–0.7oz), add the salt and mix on medium speed for a further 2 minutes until all the salt has been combined.
6. Stop the mixer and let the dough rest for 5 minutes.
7. Restart the mixer on slow speed and add the oil gradually until it's all combined.
8. Allow the dough to rest for 5 minutes before removing from the mixer. If you wish to freeze any dough, after removing it from the mixer, divide it into desired portions and freeze it before it begins fermenting.
9. Form the dough into a big ball. Place in a bowl, cover and put into the fridge for 12–24 hours.
10. Remove from the fridge, divide and shape the dough into 550g (19.4oz) dough balls, then transfer to a dough tray and cover. Leave at room temperature for 3 hours or until the balls have doubled in size (time will vary based on the room temperature).
11. Transfer to an oiled pizza pan – see page 54 on 'How to Make a Pan Pizza'.

Tips

This is a high-hydration dough. To avoid the dough sticking to your hands, wet them first. Use a bench scraper to help form the dough into a ball.

Preferment: Poolish

Poolish is a popular preferment used in pizza dough and breads such as New York-style and pan pizza. It's a liquid preferment that looks a little like a sourdough starter, but it's made of equal parts flour, water and a tiny bit of yeast. It helps to bring flavour to your dough as well as thin, crispy crusts. Recipes will quote the amount of poolish in baker's percentages. Generally, it's around 10–20% of poolish used in each recipe. For example, if a recipe has 1000g (35.3oz) total flour, add 200g (7oz) poolish for 20%.

Prep Time
5 mins

Proof Time
12-16 hours

Makes
150g (5.3oz) of preferment -
scale up or down as necessary

75g (2.6oz) cold water
0.2g (0.007oz) instant or
   active dried yeast
75g (2.6oz) strong bread flour

1. Combine all the ingredients in a small bowl and mix together with a spatula until there is no dry flour left.
2. Cover and allow to sit at room temperature between 18–20°C (64–68°F) for 12–16 hours. Once the preferment has doubled in volume it is ready to use in a recipe.

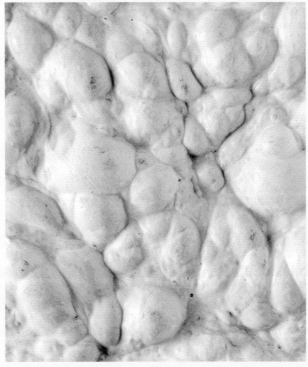

Preferment: Biga

Biga is often used in high-hydration doughs like focaccia where you want a light and airy crumb. It's a low-hydration preferment meaning it's not equal parts flour and water, giving it a dry consistency.

Prep Time
15 mins

_____

750g (26.5oz) strong bread flour
375g (13.2oz) cold water
4g (0.15oz) instant or
   active dry yeast

Proof Time
16 hours

Makes
Makes 150g (5.3oz) of
preferment – scale up
or down as necessary

1. Add the water and the yeast to a plastic container or a large bowl and mix until all the yeast has dissolved.
2. Add the flour and mix by hand until the mixture has a dry, lumpy consistency (so there's no dry flour left). Cover with cling film or a lid and leave at a room temperature of around 18°C (64°F) for 4 hours before transferring to the fridge for a further 12 hours.

Preferment: Sourdough Starter

Sourdough starters have been used for thousands of years to leaven breads and unlike biga and poolish, sourdough does not use commercial yeast. It's a great next step to explore once you've mastered a foundational pizza dough and adds a unique flavour.

A starter becomes active thanks to naturally occurring microbes (including several yeast strains) in the air. Combining water and flour is building a home for the helpful microbes to live.

Once your starter is established, you can keep it in the fridge and simply feed it once a week to keep it happy and healthy.

A starter can take as little as 6 days to over 2 weeks to make, depending on the surrounding conditions.

Makes

```
Makes 150g (5.3oz) of preferment -
scale up or down as necessary
```

```
260g (9.2oz) rye flour
   (light or dark)
280g (9.5oz) room-temperature water
```

```
Tips

Once your starter is
established, you only
need to feed it once or
twice before using it
in a recipe. Otherwise,
store it in the fridge
and feed it every 2
weeks to keep it happy
and healthy.
```

1. **Day 1:** Add 100g (3.5oz) water and 100g (3.5oz) rye flour to a clean jar. Use a spoon or spatula to stir until well combined, then loosely cover with a lid. Leave the mixture for 24 hours at room temperature (18–20°C/64–68°F).
2. **Days 2–4:** Transfer 75g (2.6oz) of the mixture into a second jar (this is called a discard). In the original jar, stir in 120g (4.2oz) water to evenly loosen the mixture, then stir in 100g (3.5oz) rye flour until well incorporated. Place a rubber band to the height of the mixture in the jar, to make it easy to spot any changes in volume and leave loosely covered with the jar lid for 24 hours again in a warm place. Repeat every day for 3 more days.
3. **Day 5 onwards:** Remove half of the starter, add 60g (2.1oz) of water and stir to mix, then add 60g (2.1oz) of flour. Keep feeding your starter every day until it starts to double in size. Depending on your environment, you will start to see your starter double in size any day from Day 6 to Day 14.
4. Once your starter doubles in size you can use it to bake sourdough recipes.

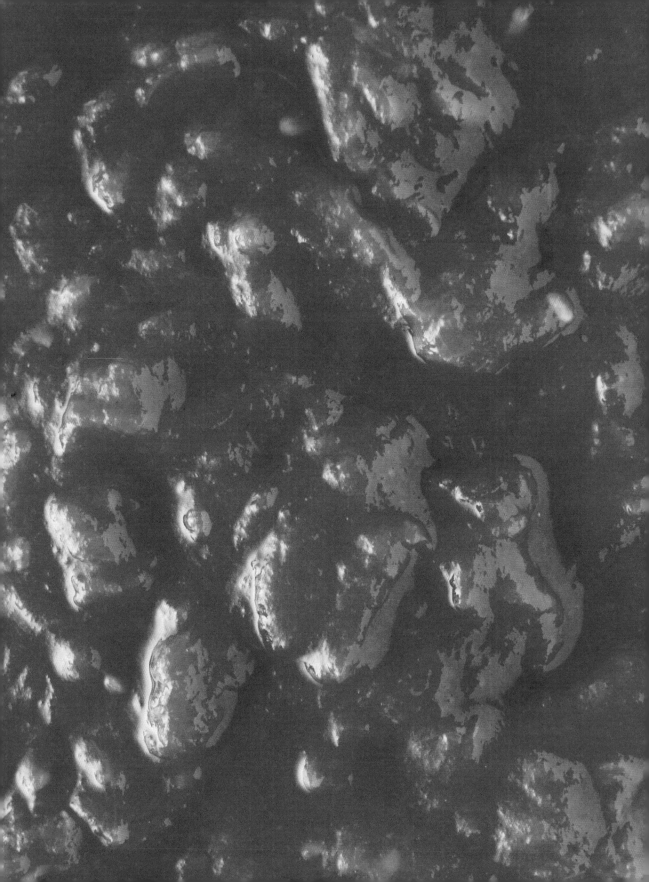

04

Sauces, Dips & Toppings

Simple Tomato Sauce

For us, this is all about good ingredients and simplicity. It's worth getting the best tomatoes you can find here, as flavour is key.

Prep Time
5 mins

_____

800g (28oz) tinned whole
    peeled tomatoes
5g (0.2oz) fine sea salt

Makes
Makes: 800g (28oz)
(enough for about 10 pizzas)

1. Remove and discard the cores from the tomatoes and place the tomatoes into a bowl, reserving the tomato juice left in the tin.
2. Use an immersion blender to pulse-blend the cored tomatoes to the desired consistency, then fold the reserved tomato juice into the tomatoes. Season with the salt. The finished sauce should have some texture to it.

Tips

Use high-quality tinned tomatoes. We recommend Bianco Di Napoli tinned tomatoes from our friend Chris Bianco, or similar. The better the tomato, the better the sauce.

Marinara Sauce

The addition of garlic, olive oil and oregano give this sauce great depth. We love to use it on our Detroit-style pizzas.

Prep Time
10 mins

Makes
800g (28oz) (enough for about 10 pizzas)

800g (28oz) tinned whole
   peeled tomatoes
2g (0.07oz) flaky sea salt
30ml (1fl oz) olive oil
12g (0.4oz) garlic cloves, peeled
1 tsp dried oregano

1. Remove and discard the cores from the tomatoes and place the tomatoes into a bowl, reserving the tomato juice left in the tin.
2. In a separate bowl, add the salt, olive oil, garlic and oregano to the reserved tomato juice and use an immersion blender to blend until smooth.
3. Pulse-blend the cored tomatoes until they are well blended but still with a little texture, then stir the tomato juice into the pulsed tomatoes.

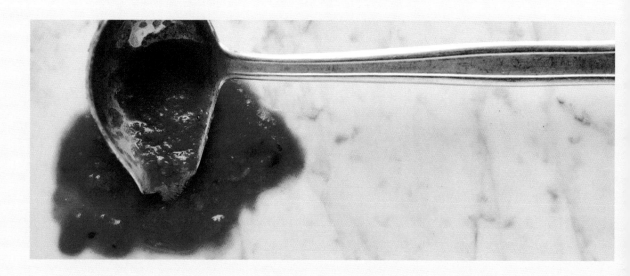

Garlic in Oil

This works great as a base for Pizza Bianca (page 119). Simply put, it's oil infused with garlic.

Prep Time
50 mins

Makes
150g (5.3oz) (enough for about 6 pizzas)

50g (1.8oz) garlic cloves, peeled
100ml (3.5fl oz) extra virgin olive oil

1. Thinly slice the garlic (for best results use a mandoline), then add it to the olive oil and allow it to steep at room temperature for at least a few hours before using. For best results, let the garlic steep for up to 24 hours.

Vodka Sauce

Traditionally this sauce is used in American-Italian pasta dishes, but it works great on pizzas too. A creamy tomato sauce with the vodka bringing an additional kick of flavour.

Prep Time
5 mins

Cook Time
20 mins

Makes
933g (33oz) (enough for about 12 pizzas)

45ml (1.6fl oz) olive oil

55g (1.9oz) shallots, chopped

2g (.07oz) garlic cloves, chopped

75ml (2.6fl oz) vodka

500g (17.6oz) crushed tinned tomatoes

½ tsp dried oregano

200ml (7fl oz) double (heavy) cream

55g (1.9oz) Pecorino Romano, grated

1g (.05oz) flaky sea salt

1. Heat the olive oil in a saucepan over a medium heat, then add the shallots and garlic and sweat until translucent and aromatic, but not browned.
2. Carefully pour the vodka into the pan and ignite with a flame to cook out the alcohol. Add the crushed tomatoes and dried oregano and cook for 2–3 minutes to reduce, then add the cream to the pan and bring to a simmer. Using an immersion blender, blend the sauce until smooth, then stir in grated Pecorino Romano and salt and simmer for 5–10 minutes, until it reaches a thick enough consistency to coat the back of a spoon.

Roasted Tomato Sauce

Rich roasted tomatoes. A great alternative to our Simple Tomato Sauce (page 82).

Prep Time
5 mins

Cook Time
20 mins

Makes
933g (33oz) (enough for about 12 pizzas)

500g (17.6oz) ripe cherry
  tomatoes
25g (0.9oz) garlic cloves, peeled
100g (3.5oz) white onion,
  roughly chopped
75ml (2.6fl oz) extra virgin
  olive oil
1 tsp dried oregano
1 tsp flaky sea salt
¼ tsp dried chilli flakes
¼ tsp freshly ground black
  pepper
4-6 basil leaves

1. Preheat your pizza oven to 200°C/400°F (stone floor temperature).
2. Place all the ingredients in a baking dish, mix well, then roast in the oven for 25 minutes.
3. After roasting, allow the vegetables to rest for 5 minutes before pulsing in a blender until you have a sauce with a little texture in it. Chill overnight in the fridge for the best results!

Hot
Honey

Sweet heat. This is an essential sauce for your modern pizza tool kit and it's a great addition to any pizza. Experiment with different kinds of chilli flakes to create varied flavours of hot honey.

Prep Time
4 mins

Cook Time
20 mins

Makes
50g (8.8oz)

_____

250g (8.8oz) clear honey
1 tbsp dried chilli flakes

1. Gently heat the honey and chilli flakes in a small saucepan over a medium heat.
2. Remove the pan from heat once small bubbles form on the edges of the pan and set aside to cool. Store in a glass jar at room temperature.
3. Leave the chilli flakes in so the spiciness builds over time, or strain the honey through a fine-mesh sieve.
4. The honey will keep for up to 3 months in a sterilised jar, stored in a cool, dark place.

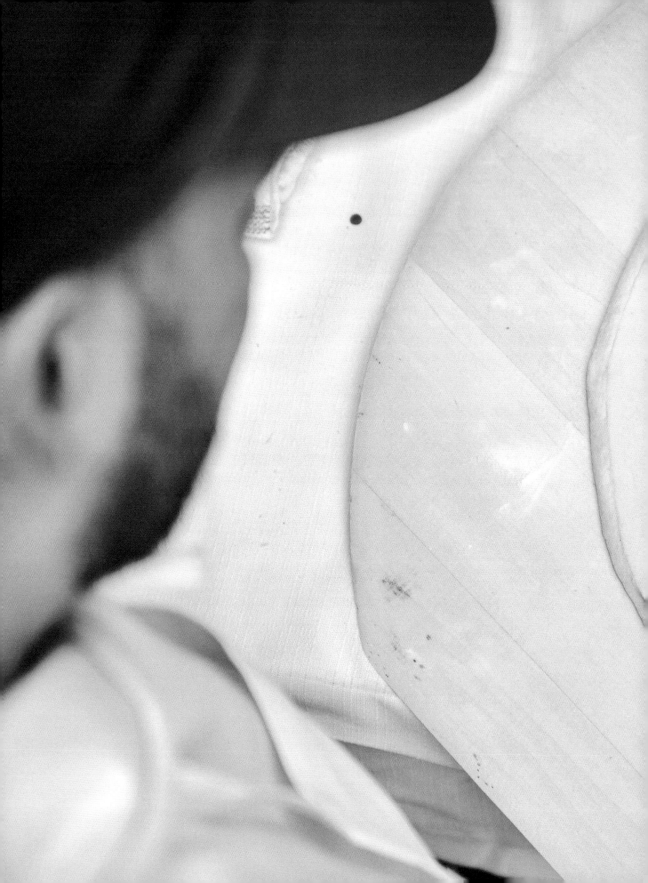

Anchovy Sauce

For those that love salty flavours. An intense rich sauce that's great for dipping.

Prep Time
5 mins

Cook Time
10 mins

Makes
450g (15.8oz) (enough for about 6 pizzas)

---

1 x 400g (14oz) tin plum tomatoes
50ml (1.7fl oz) extra virgin
   olive oil
4 garlic cloves, crushed
50g (1.8oz) anchovies in olive oil
Flaky sea salt (optional)

1. Tip the plum tomatoes into a bowl and crush them with your hands or a fork.
2. Heat the oil in a frying pan over a medium heat and add the garlic, then the anchovies and their oil. Cook for a few minutes until the garlic is soft and fragrant and the anchovies have broken up, then add the crushed tomatoes and leave to bubble for 5 minutes, stirring every so often, until the sauce has thickened.
3. Taste and season with a little salt if needed, then blend with an immersion blender until smooth. Leave to cool and keep in the fridge for up to 1 week.

Spicy Ranch

Bringing together two of our great loves – ranch and sriracha. Perfect for dipping.

Prep Time
5 mins

Makes
500g (17.6oz) (enough for
about 6 pizzas)

120g (4.2oz) mayonnaise
120g (4.2oz) soured cream
100ml (3.5fl oz) buttermilk
½ tsp dried dill
⅓ tsp dried parsley
1 tsp dried chives
¼ tsp onion powder
½ tsp garlic powder
1 tbsp white wine vinegar
150g (5.3oz) sriracha

1. Whisk all of the ingredients together in a bowl and season to
   taste (leave out the sriracha for a traditional ranch dressing).
   Add a little extra vinegar for extra sharpness and use more or
   less sriracha depending on how hot you want it. Cover and leave
   in the fridge for a few hours to firm up a little before using. Your
   spicy ranch will keep in the fridge for up to 1 week.

Basil Pesto

Our take on the traditional pesto – it's great for dipping or as an alternative base to tomato. If you're feeling adventurous, try switching the basil with something different like watercress, kale or wild garlic.

Prep Time
10 mins

Makes
333g (11.7oz) (enough for about 4 pizzas)

50g (1.8oz) fresh basil, thick stems removed

100ml (3.5fl oz) extra virgin olive oil

50g (1.8oz) pine nuts

4g (.15oz) garlic cloves

3g (.10oz) flaky sea salt

1g (.05oz) freshly ground black pepper

50g (1.8oz) Pecorino Romano, grated

75ml (2.6fl oz) cold water

1. Blanch the basil by putting the basil into a sieve and plunging it into a pan of boiling water for 15 seconds. Push the leaves down into the water and stir them so that they blanch evenly, then plunge into ice water.

2. Using an immersion blender, blend the oil, pine nuts, garlic, salt and pepper until smooth, then add the blanched basil and blend again until smooth.

3. Add the grated Pecorino Romano and blend until smooth, then while still blending, gradually add the cold water – this gives the pesto a silky texture.

4. Cover and keep refrigerated for up to a week.

Jalapeño Pesto

A spicy alternative to a traditional pesto. Again, use for dipping or as a base when you want to let the world know you're not afraid to be a little wild.

Prep Time
10 mins

Makes
400g (14oz) (enough for about 5 pizzas)

---

2 garlic cloves, peeled
4 fresh jalapeños, roughly
  chopped
60g (2.1oz) walnuts
60g (2.1oz) Parmigiano Reggiano,
  grated
100g (3.5oz) basil,
  thick stems removed
120ml (4fl oz) extra virgin
  olive oil
Flaky sea salt
Freshly ground black pepper

1. Put the garlic, jalapeños, walnuts and Parmigiano Reggiano in a small food processor and blend until you have a well-combined paste. (You may want to add extra chillies here if you'd like your pesto super spicy.)

2. Add the basil leaves and pulse until they are roughly chopped through the mixture. Add the oil bit by bit, blending for a second or so each time until the pesto has a spoonable consistency. You may not need all the oil, and be careful not to over-process the pesto, otherwise the basil can turn a little bitter. Season to taste with salt and pepper.

3. The pesto will keep for at least a week in the fridge if you keep it covered with oil.

Chilli Sauce

Brings the heat for the spice lovers. Great for dipping or drizzling over your pizza.

Prep Time
5 mins

Cook Time
5 mins

Makes
450g (15.8oz) (enough for about 6 pizzas)

---

3 red chillies
1 x 400g (14oz) tin plum tomatoes
1 tbsp red wine vinegar
1 tbsp caster (superfine) sugar
2 tbsp olive oil
Flaky sea salt

Tips

You can deseed the chillies if you like but it's not necessary. If you're worried about it being too spicy you could always add fewer chillies or a milder variety.

1. When your pizza oven is hot from cooking something else, place the red chillies on the floor of the oven near the heat source and allow them to char a little all over, then leave to cool.
2. Roughly chop the chillies, discarding the stems, then simply blend them with the rest of the ingredients.
3. Transfer the sauce to a small saucepan and simmer gently until it has thickened.
4. Taste and add extra salt, vinegar and sugar as you see fit, then transfer to a sterilised jar. Keep in the fridge for up to 5 days.

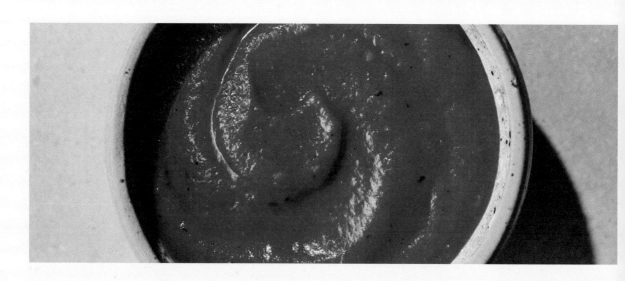

Garlic Cream

Garlicy and creamy. What's not to love? Great for dipping or drizzling over your pizza.

Prep Time
5 mins

Cook Time
5 mins

Makes
812g (28.6oz) (enough for about 10 pizzas)

100g (3.5oz) plain (all-purpose) flour or '00' flour
500ml (16.9fl oz) water
1 tbsp extra virgin olive oil
30g (1oz) garlic cloves, peeled
150g (5.3oz) Pecorino Romano, grated
½ tsp ground white pepper

1. Whisk the flour and water together in a bowl and set to one side.
2. Heat the olive oil in a saucepan over a medium heat. Use a microplane grater to grate the garlic into the oil and sauté for a minute or so until aromatic. Reduce the heat to low, pour the water and flour mixture into the pan and whisk to begin making a smooth roux. Allow the roux to rise to a gentle simmer, then remove from heat and allow it to cool down to room temperature.
3. Using an immersion blender or countertop blender, blend the Pecorino Romano, white pepper and cooled roux until the mixture has a silky-smooth consistency. Chill overnight in the fridge for the best results and use within 3 days.

Crispy Onions

Bringing that crunch and textural diversity to your pizza.

Prep Time
5 mins

Cook Time
5 mins

150ml (5fl oz) neutral-flavoured
  oil (e.g., sunflower,
  vegetable, grapeseed)
4 shallots, peeled and very
  thinly sliced

1. Heat the oil in a small frying pan over a medium heat to 140°C (284°F), then gently lower the sliced shallots into the oil with a spoon and gently move them into one even layer in the oil.
2. Fry the shallots for 3–5 minutes until golden brown, then use a slotted spoon to remove them from the oil and place them on a paper towel-lined plate. Leave them to cool completely before storing in an airtight container. Your crispy onions will keep well for up to 1 week.

Confit Garlic

Here, garlic is slow-cooked in fat until it caramelises and becomes soft and golden. Confit garlic has a less intense, sweeter flavour than raw garlic and is a tasty pizza topping.

Prep Time
5 mins

Cook Time
2 hours

3 garlic bulbs, cloves separated
  and peeled
200ml (6.7fl oz) olive oil
Flaky sea salt
Freshly ground black pepper

1. Preheat your pizza oven to 110°C (230°F) (stone floor temperature).
2. Put the garlic cloves in a small baking tray and pour over the oil (you want to make sure the oil fully covers the garlic cloves). Season well with salt and pepper and slow roast the garlic in the oven for about 2 hours until the cloves are soft and a light golden colour.
3. Remove from the oven and leave them to cool to room temperature, then store in a clean airtight container, making sure they are covered in the oil (add a little extra if needed).
4. If kept in a sterilised jar covered in oil, your garlic will keep for up to 2–3 months in the fridge.

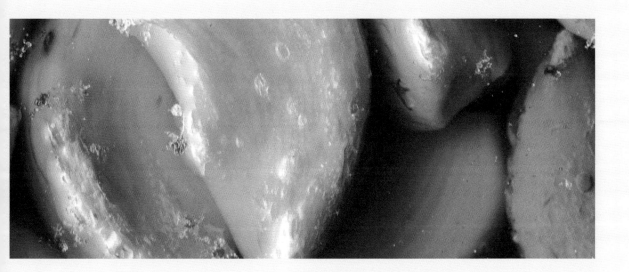

Confit Tomatoes

Traditional pizza flavour gets the volume turned up. This is a great way to use up some leftover cherry tomatoes and add an extra pop to your pizza toppings.

Prep Time
5 mins

Cook Time
2 hours

450g (16oz) cherry tomatoes
A few sprigs of thyme
200ml (6.7fl oz) extra virgin
  olive oil
Flaky sea salt
Freshly ground black pepper

1. Preheat your pizza oven to 110°C (230°F) (stone floor temperature).
2. Put the tomatoes in a deep baking tray or dish, then nestle in the thyme and pour over the oil (you want to make sure the oil covers the tomatoes by a third or half). Season well with salt and pepper.
3. Slow roast the tomatoes in the oven for about 2 hours until they are wrinkly and a few have burst.
4. Remove from the oven and leave the tomatoes to cool to room temperature, then store in a clean airtight container, making sure they are covered in the oil (add a little extra oil if needed). If kept in a sterilised jar covered in oil, the tomatoes will keep for up to 2–3 weeks in the fridge.

Candied Jalapeños

Sweet and spicy. A playful addition to any pizza.

Prep Time
20 mins

Cook Time
15 mins

250ml (8.4fl oz) cider vinegar
180g (6.3oz) caster (superfine)
  or granulated sugar
½ tsp celery seeds
1 tsp garlic powder
½ tsp cayenne pepper
250g (8.8oz) fresh green
  jalapeños, cut into
  5mm-(0.2in-) thick slices

1. Bring the vinegar, sugar, celery seeds, garlic powder and cayenne pepper to the boil in a small saucepan, then reduce the heat and simmer for 5 minutes until the liquid has thickened a little.
2. Add the sliced jalapeños and simmer for 5 more minutes until the chillies have softened slightly.
3. Use a slotted spoon to transfer the chillies to a sterilised jar, then boil the remaining liquid for another 5 minutes until you have a syrup.
4. Pour the syrup over the jalapeños, making sure they are all covered, then seal the jar and place in the fridge for a week or so to allow the flavours to develop. (You can leave them for just a few hours if you're feeling impatient, but they will get better with a little extra chilling.)
5. Keep them in the fridge and eat them within 2 months.

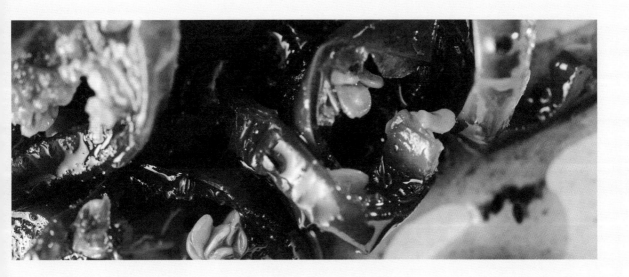

Pickled
Red Onions

A vibrant addition to any pizza. The tang of the onions is an excellent way to add acidity. This method can work for pickling any veg.

Prep Time
5 mins, plus pickling time

_____

2 red onions, thinly sliced

1 tsp black peppercorns

150ml (5fl oz) white wine vinegar

150ml (5fl oz) water

30g (1oz) caster (superfine) sugar

1 tsp salt

1. Place the onions and peppercorns in a clean jar and set to one side.
2. Heat the vinegar and water in a small saucepan, add the sugar and salt and stir until dissolved. Pour the mixture over the sliced onions in the jar and leave to cool.
3. The onions should take about 30 minutes to turn bright pink, then they're ready to eat.
4. Keep the onions in a sterilised glass jar and they will keep in the fridge for about 2 weeks.

Tips

You can also follow this method to pickle jalapeños. Just thinly slice 6 chillies and use instead of the red onions.

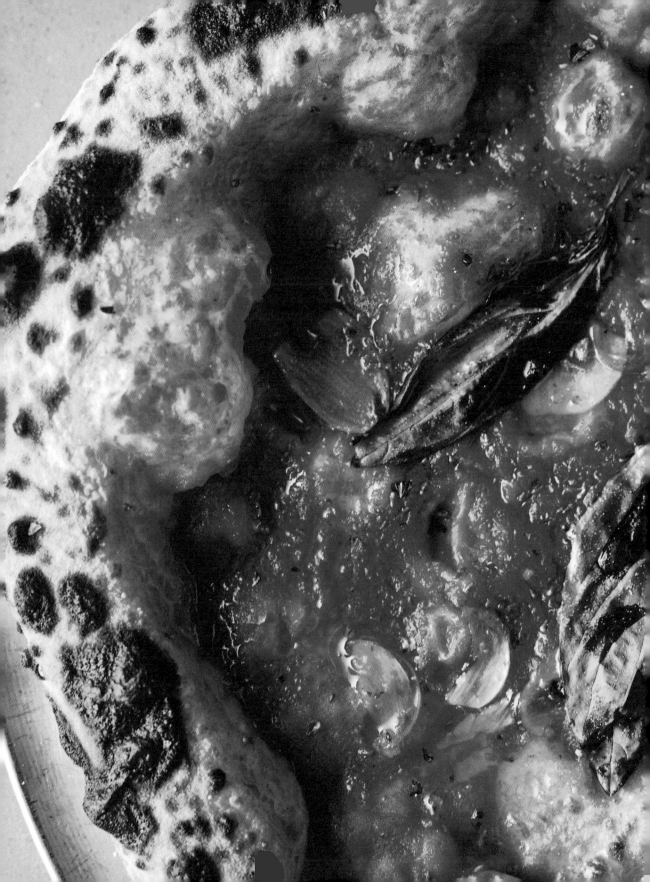

05 Pizza

Everyone loves pizza. Some say the combination of savoury crust, the sauce and fat from the cheese makes for the perfect food. With Gozney, you can create your own epic pizza at home. Friends, family, and even kids can get in on the action. There's rigid tradition and creative exploration when it comes to pizza-making, and both have a place in the Gozney pizza universe. Pizza can be a refined culinary craft or a pizza party in the garden. Whatever your approach to pizza, it's the right approach. Our pizza recipes are intended to give you a range of tried and tested combinations of ingredients that inspire you to find your own pizza path.

How to use this recipe section:

We've broken up this recipe section by recommended dough and pizza types. As much as some people might tell you there's one, single right way to make pizza, we don't agree. Pizza is expressive. Take any of the following recipes and use any of our pizza dough recipes and combine them with the different topping methods as your guide. So, if it's a Neapolitan recipe why not try it with New York-style dough. Go wild and enjoy creating.

Richie's Upside-down Cheese Pizza

From our own Richard Preston (aka Richie P) comes one of his favourites from the Gozney kitchen. A twist on a classic cheese pizza – cheese first, sauce second.

Prep Time
10 mins

Cook Time
5 mins

Makes
1 x 14-inch pizza
(feeds 2–3 people)

---

1 x 350g (12.3oz) Signature-style
   Pizza dough ball (page 58)
100–125g (3.5–4.5oz) low-moisture
   mozzarella, cut into 1cm
   (0.4in)-thick slices
50g (1.8oz) fresh mozzarella,
   cut into 2.5cm (1in) cubes
100g (3.5oz) Simple Tomato Sauce
   (page 82)

To serve
Finely grated Pecorino Romano or
   Parmigiano Reggiano
Extra virgin olive oil,
   for drizzling

1. Preheat your pizza oven to 340°C (650°F) (stone floor temperature).
2. Press and open the dough into a 14-inch circle and place it on a lightly floured pizza peel.
3. Top the pizza with the sliced low-moisture mozzarella first, then place a few cubes of the fresh mozzarella on top. Finally, ladle over the sauce in spots in and around the cheese.
4. Launch the pizza into the oven and bake on a low flame, rotating the pizza 90 degrees every minute, for 4 minutes. Cook for a final minute with the flame on high to obtain a bit more colour, making sure to rotate the pizza frequently.
5. Place on a cooling screen or wire rack and rest for 1 minute, then cut into 6–8 pieces and finish it with finely grated Pecorino or Parmigiano and drizzle with extra virgin olive oil.

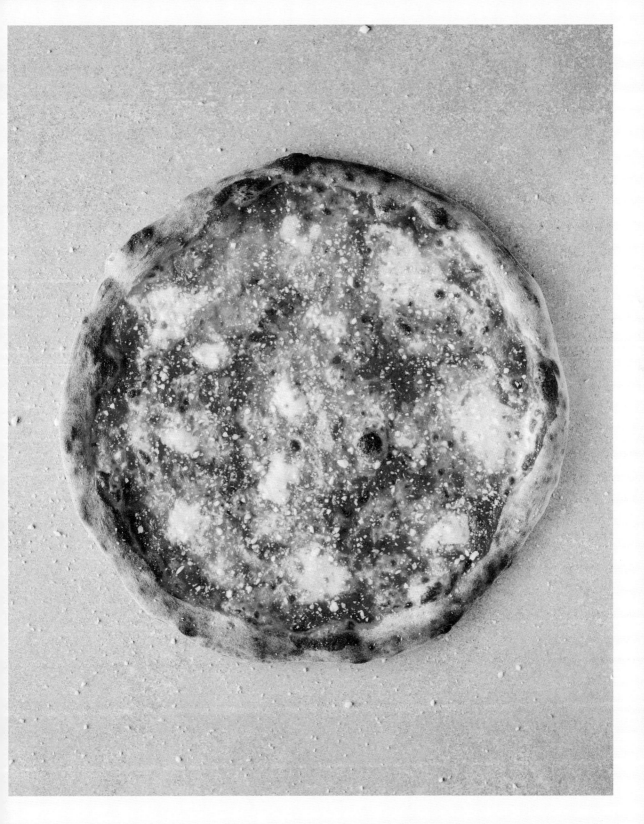

Margherita

What can we say. A household name. The classic. Margherita brings together three simple flavours – basil, tomatoes and cheese – and makes magic. Reportedly created for Queen Margherita of Savoy, the colours represent the Italian flag.

Prep Time
10 mins

Cook Time
60-90 seconds

Makes
1 x 12-inch pizzas
(feeds 1-2 people)

---

1 x 260g (9.2oz) Neapolitan-style
  Pizza dough ball (page 60)
75g (2.6oz) Simple Tomato Sauce
  (page 82)
Parmigiano Reggiano, finely grated
Basil leaves
Fior di latte mozzarella,
  cut into 1cm (0.4in) cubes
Extra virgin olive oil,
  for drizzling

1. Preheat your pizza oven to 430°C (800°F) (stone floor temperature).
2. Press and open the dough into a 12-inch circle, top with the tomato sauce, a light covering of finely grated Parmigiano Reggiano, a few basil leaves and a handful of fresh fior di latte mozzarella cubes.
3. Transfer to a lightly floured peel and redistribute any toppings as required.
4. Lightly drizzle some olive oil over the pizza, then launch it into the oven and bake on a high flame, rotating the pizza 90 degrees every 15–20 seconds. The pizza should take 60–90 seconds to cook in total.

Neapolitan-style dough

Marinara

One of the team's favourites. Super simple – tomatoes, garlic, oregano, olive oil. No cheese.

Prep Time
10 mins

Cook Time
60–90 seconds

Makes
1 x 12-inch pizza
(feeds 1–2 people)

---

1 x 260g (9.2oz) Neapolitan-style
   Pizza dough ball (page 60)
75g (2.6oz) Simple Tomato Sauce
   (page 82)
1 large garlic clove,
   thinly sliced
Pinch of dried oregano, plus
   extra to serve
Extra virgin olive oil,
   for drizzling
Basil leaves, to serve

1. Preheat your pizza oven to 430°C (800°F) (stone floor temperature).
2. Press and open the dough into a 12-inch circle, top with the tomato sauce, thinly sliced garlic and dried oregano.
3. Transfer to a lightly floured peel and redistribute any toppings as required.
4. Give the pizza a generous glug of olive oil, then launch it into the oven and bake on a high flame, rotating the pizza 90 degrees every 15–20 seconds. The pizza should take 60–90 seconds to cook in total.
5. Once baked, sprinkle with extra oregano and garnish with a few fresh basil leaves.

Roasted Mushroom Pizza Bianca

Bianca meaning 'white'. No tomato sauce. Covered in garlic oil and topped with roasted mushrooms, this pizza packs flavour. Don't underestimate a pizza without a sauce.

Prep Time
30 mins

Cook Time
60–90 seconds

Makes
1 x 12-inch pizza
(feeds 1–2 people)

---

1 x 260g (9.2oz) Neapolitan-style
  Pizza dough ball (page 60)
50g (1.8oz) ricotta
20g (0.7oz) Pecorino Romano,
  plus extra to serve
75–100g (2.6–3.5oz) fior di
  latte mozzarella, cut or torn
Parsley, roughly chopped,
  to garnish

For the mushrooms
100g (3.5oz) chestnut mushrooms
  (or mushroom of choice), sliced
15g (0.5oz) unsalted butter
Extra virgin olive oil,
  for drizzling
Flaky sea salt
2 garlic cloves, thinly sliced

1. Preheat your pizza oven to 260°C (500°F) (stone floor temperature) and heat a cast-iron pan in the oven for cooking the mushrooms.
2. When the pan is hot, add the mushrooms with the butter and a glug of olive oil. Fry in the oven for a few minutes, then add the salt and sliced garlic. Cook for a few minutes more until the mushrooms are a lovely deep golden colour, then set to one side.
3. Heat the pizza oven to 430°C (800°F) (stone floor temperature).
4. Press and open the dough into a 12-inch circle and top it with the ricotta. Grate over the Pecorino and top with the fior di latte and the mushrooms.
5. Transfer to a lightly floured peel and redistribute any toppings as required.
6. Drizzle some olive oil over the pizza, then launch it into the oven and bake on a high flame, rotating the pizza 90 degrees every 15–20 seconds. The pizza should take 60–90 seconds to cook in total.
7. Finish the pizza with chopped parsley and a little extra Pecorino Romano.

Adam's Chorizo & Manchego Pizza

A menu special from our good friend Adam Atkins, aka Peddling Pizza. Fatty chorizo and fiery teardrop peppers are balanced perfectly with a combination of buffalo mozzarella and freshly grated Manchego.

Prep Time
10 mins

Cook Time
60–90 seconds

Makes
1 x 12-inch pizza
(feeds 1-2 people)

---

1 x 260g (9.2oz) Neapolitan-style Pizza dough ball (page 60)

80g (2.8oz) Simple Tomato Sauce (page 82)

10g (0.3oz) Pecorino Romano, grated

A few fresh basil leaves, torn

75-100g (2.6-3.5oz) fior di latte mozzarella, cubed or torn

Needles from a sprig of rosemary

50g (1.8oz) sliced chorizo

8-10 pickled teardrop peppers

Extra virgin olive oil, for drizzling

10g (0.3oz) Manchego, grated

1. Preheat your pizza oven to 430°C (800°F) (stone floor temperature).
2. Press and open the dough into a 12-inch circle, top it with the tomato sauce, grated Pecorino Romano, basil, fior di latte, rosemary needles, chorizo and teardrop peppers.
3. Transfer to a lightly floured peel and redistribute any toppings as required.
4. Drizzle some olive oil over the pizza, then launch it into the oven and bake on a high flame, rotating the pizza 90 degrees every 15–20 seconds. The pizza should take 60–90 seconds to cook in total.
5. Once baked, sprinkle with the grated Manchego.

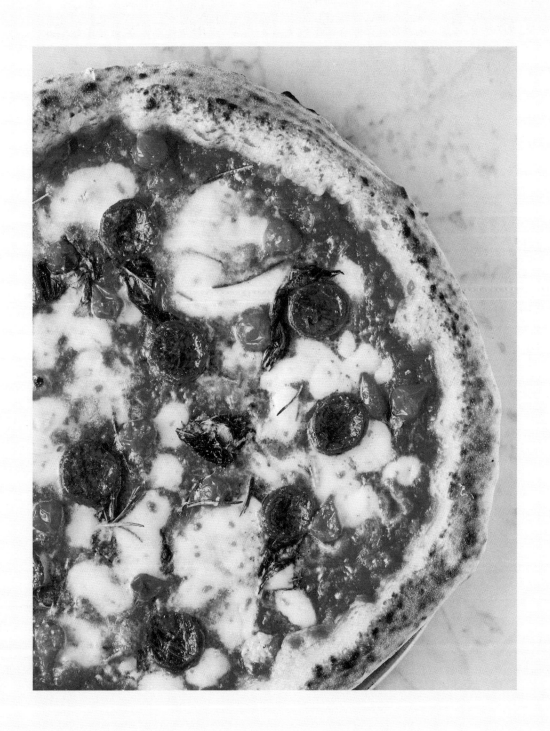

Tom's Signature Marmite & Hot Honey Pizza

What's become Tom Gozney's signature, almost to his reluctance. Birthed from long nights messing about in the kitchen. A take on the classic English flavour profile, Marmite on toast, but elevated to the art of pizza.

Prep Time
10 mins

Cook Time
60-90 seconds

Makes
1 x 12-inch pizza
(feeds 1-2 people)

---

1 x 270g (9.5oz) Tom's 96-Hour
 Pizza dough ball (page 62)
100-125g (3.5-4.5oz) low-moisture
 mozzarella, shredded
4 tsp Marmite
Extra virgin olive oil,
 for drizzling

To serve
Crispy Onions (page 102)
Hot Honey (page 89)

1. Preheat your pizza oven to 450°C (850°F) (stone floor temperature).
2. Press and open the dough into a 12-inch circle, top it with the shredded mozzarella, a drizzle of Marmite (1 teaspoon per pizza) and add a drizzle of olive oil.
3. Transfer to a lightly floured peel and redistribute any toppings as required.
4. Launch the pizza into the oven and bake on a high flame, rotating the pizza 90 degrees every 15-20 seconds. The pizza should take 60-90 seconds to cook in total.
5. Once baked, garnish with crispy onions and drizzle with hot honey.

Tips

Warming the Marmite through first will make it easier to drizzle over the pizza.

Meatball & Cavolo Nero Pizza

Another one of Tom Gozney's favourites. A rich and hearty pizza uniting two classic Italian flavours.

Prep Time
1 hour

Cook Time
60-90 seconds

Makes
1 x 12-inch pizza
(feeds 1-2 people)

---

1 x 270g (9.5oz) Tom's 96-Hour
    Pizza dough ball (page 62)
6-8 Confit Garlic cloves
    (page 103)
100-125g (3.5-4.5oz) aged
    Provolone, cut into 1cm (0.4in)
    cubes
75-100g (2.6-3.5oz) cooked
    meatballs (page 197), crumbled
50-75g (1.8-2.6oz) cavolo nero,
    leaves torn and blanched
Extra virgin olive oil,
    for drizzling

To serve
Dried oregano
Pecorino Romano

1. Preheat your pizza oven to 450°C (850°F) (stone floor temperature).
2. Press and open the dough into a 12-inch circle and top it with torn confit garlic, aged provolone, meatballs and cavolo nero.
3. Transfer to a lightly floured peel and redistribute any toppings as required.
4. Drizzle over some extra virgin olive oil, launch the pizza into the oven and bake on a high flame, rotating the pizza 90 degrees every 15-20 seconds. The pizza should take 60-90 seconds to cook in total.
5. Once baked, sprinkle with some dried oregano and grated Pecorino Romano and drizzle with a little more extra virgin olive oil.

Anchovy, Oregano & Caper Pizza

A marinara pizza taken to the next level. One for anchovy lovers.

Prep Time
10 mins

Cook Time
60-90 seconds

Makes
1 x 12-inch pizza
(feeds 1-2 people)

---

1 x 270g (9.5oz) Tom's 96-Hour
    Pizza dough ball (page 62)
75g (2.6oz) Simple Tomato Sauce
    (page 82)
½ tsp dried oregano
1-2 garlic cloves, very thinly
    sliced and steeped in oil
    (see Garlic in Oil, page 85)
1 tbsp capers
Extra virgin olive oil,
    for drizzling

To serve
A few oregano leaves
Flaky sea salt
4-6 tinned white anchovy fillets

1. Preheat your pizza oven to 450°C (850°F) (stone floor temperature).
2. Press and open the dough into a 12-inch circle, then top it with the tomato sauce, dried oregano, sliced garlic and capers.
3. Transfer to a lightly floured peel and redistribute any toppings as required.
4. Drizzle over some extra virgin olive oil, launch the pizza into the oven and bake on a high flame, rotating the pizza 90 degrees every 15–20 seconds. The pizza should take 60–90 seconds to cook in total.
5. Once baked, top with oregano leaves, a pinch of sea salt flakes, the anchovy fillets and a little more extra virgin olive oil.

Chilli Crisp Pizza

Our founder, Tom Gozney, is a big fan of combining textures and umami flavours. Crunchy, spicy and delicious. This pizza packs a punch.

Prep Time
10 mins

Cook Time
60–90 seconds

Makes
1 x 12-inch pizza
(feeds 1–2 people)

---

1 x 270g (9.5oz) Tom's 96-Hour
  Pizza dough ball (page 62)
1-2 garlic cloves, very thinly
  sliced and steeped in oil (see
  Garlic in Oil, page 85)
100-125g (3.5-4.5oz) fresh
  mozzarella, cut into 1cm
  (0.4in) cubes

To serve
¼ red onion, thinly sliced
1-2 tsp crispy chilli in oil
  (from a jar)
Grated Parmigiano Reggiano

1. Preheat your pizza oven to 450°C (850°F) stone floor temperature.

2. Press and open the dough into a 12-inch circle and top it with the sliced garlic and a drizzle of the garlic oil followed by the mozzarella.

3. Transfer to a lightly floured peel and redistribute any toppings as required.

4. Launch the pizza into the oven and bake on a high flame, rotating the pizza 90 degrees every 15–20 seconds. The pizza should take 60–90 seconds to cook in total.

5. Once baked, finish with the sliced red onion, chilli crisp and plenty of grated Parmigiano Reggiano.

Feng's Pizza Caprese

Feng Chen, aka Leopard Crust, has been a part of the Gozney family for years and is the queen of imaginative pizzas. However, the simplicity of this pizza is the perfect way to showcase ingredients at their peak. Using the highest-quality tomatoes and mozzarella available to you will make this pizza a true summer favourite.

Prep Time
30 mins

Cook Time
2 mins

Makes
1 x 12-inch pizza
(feeds 1-2 people)

---

1 large tomato (heirloom, optional)
1 x 270g (9.5oz) Sourdough Pizza dough ball (page 66)
Extra virgin olive oil, for drizzling
Flaky sea salt and freshly ground black pepper

To serve
200g (7oz) buffalo mozzarella, torn
Fresh basil leaves

1. Preheat your pizza oven to 450°C (850°F) (stone floor temperature).
2. Use a serrated knife to thinly slice the tomato, then arrange slices in a single layer on a sheet of paper towel. Season with salt, then use another paper towel to remove excess moisture. Transfer the tomato slices to a bowl, sprinkle with salt and pepper, then coat generously in extra virgin olive oil.
3. Press and open the dough into a 12-inch circle and top it with the sliced tomatoes. Save the remaining olive oil in the bowl as a post-bake topping.
4. Transfer to a lightly floured peel, then launch the pizza into the oven and bake on a medium flame for 1½–2 minutes, rotating the pizza 90 degrees every 20–30 seconds.
5. Once baked, top with the torn buffalo mozzarella and basil leaves, then season lightly with salt and pepper before spooning over the leftover extra virgin olive oil used for the tomatoes.

Ines' Salad Pizza ft. Gabagool

Private chef and pizza mentor, Ines Barlerin Glaser, aka Lupa Cotta, brings the free-living, healthy spirit of California to Neapolitan pizza. Featuring the Italian-American classic cold-cut capicola, otherwise known as gabagool. Stacked with goodness, try her salad pizza with a bite of sunshine (real sunshine not required).

Prep Time
30 mins

Cook Time
60–90 seconds

Makes
1 x 12-inch pizza
(feeds 1–2 people)

---

1 x 260g (9.2oz) Neapolitan-style
  Pizza dough ball (page 60)
60–80g (2.1–2.8oz) shredded sharp
  provolone
4 slices of capicola (coppa),
  also known as gabagool
$\frac{1}{4}$ red onion, thinly sliced

To serve
Hot Honey (page 89),
  for drizzling
Pinch of dried oregano
1 burrata, torn
A large handful of hearty Italian
  salad greens
4–5 pickled peppadews, torn
A few parsley leaves
Juice of $\frac{1}{2}$ lemon
2 tsp extra virgin olive oil
Flaky sea salt
Shaved Pecorino Romano, to taste

1. **Preheat your pizza oven to 450°C (850°F) (stone floor temperature).**
2. **Press and open the dough into a 12-inch circle and top it with the shredded provolone, capicola and most of the thinly sliced onion.**
3. **Transfer to a lightly floured peel and redistribute any toppings as required.**
4. **Launch the pizza into the oven and bake on a high flame, rotating the pizza 90 degrees every 15–20 seconds. The pizza should take 60–90 seconds to cook in total.**
5. **Once baked, drizzle some hot honey over the pizza, scatter over the oregano and tear over the burrata. Toss the salad leaves, the pickled peppadews, parsley and remaining red onion with the lemon juice, olive oil and salt, then add to your pizza before finishing with some shaved Pecorino Romano.**

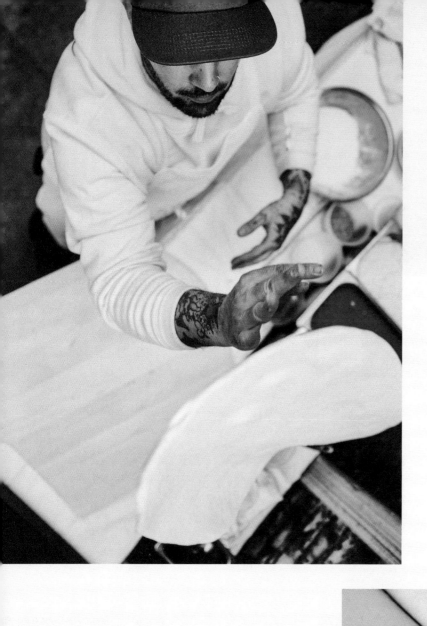
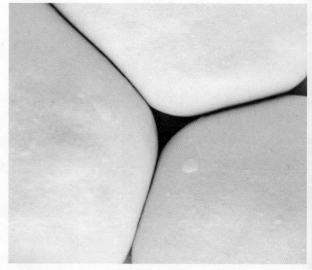

NY-style Plain Cheese Pizza

A Gozney take on an American tradition. One to impress even your most die-hard pizza friends. This is a cult classic with nothing to hide behind. Cheesy. Crispy. Goodness.

Prep Time
10 mins

Cook Time
5 mins

Makes
1 x 14-inch pizza
(feeds 2-3 people)

_____

1 x 350g (12.3oz) New York-style
   Pizza dough ball (page 64)
120g (4.2oz) Simple Tomato Sauce
   (page 82)
100–125g (3.5–4.5oz) aged
   mozzarella, shredded
35–45g (1–1.6oz) fresh
   mozzarella, cubed
Extra virgin olive oil,
   for drizzling

1. **Preheat your pizza oven to 340°C (650°F) (stone floor temperature).**
2. **Press and open the dough into a 14-inch circle and place on a lightly floured pizza peel.**
3. **Top the pizza with the tomato sauce, aged mozzarella, fresh mozzarella and a drizzle of olive oil.**
4. **Launch the pizza into the oven and bake on a low flame, rotating the pizza 90 degrees every minute, for 4 minutes. Cook for a final minute with the flame on high to obtain a bit more colour, making sure to rotate the pizza frequently.**
5. **Once baked, place on a cooling screen or wire rack and rest for 1 minute, then cut into 6–8 slices and enjoy!**

Frank's NY-style White Pie

Frank Pinello, the mastermind behind the Williamsburg pizza institution, Best Pizza, brings you one of his classics. Nothing beats getting a slice at the shop but if you can't get there, you can now make one of his signature pies at home.

Prep Time
10 mins

Cook Time
5 mins

Makes
1 x 12-inch pizza
(feeds 1–2 people)

50g (1.8oz) ricotta

2 tsp extra virgin olive oil, plus extra for drizzling

Juice of $\frac{1}{2}$ lemon

1 x 350g (12.3oz) New York-style Pizza dough ball (page 64)

2 tsp toasted sesame seeds

100g (3.5oz) low-moisture mozzarella, shredded

40g (1.4oz) caramelised onions

Flaky sea salt and freshly ground black pepper

To serve

Small handful of chopped parsley

Plenty of shaved Pecorino Romano

1. Preheat your pizza oven to 340°C (650°F) (stone floor temperature).
2. In a small bowl, mix together the ricotta, extra virgin olive oil and lemon juice with a good pinch each of salt and pepper.
3. Press and open the dough into a 12-inch circle. Use a pastry brush to lightly wet the outside edge of the dough, then gently press the sesame seeds onto it and transfer the base to a lightly floured peel. Top with the mozzarella, even dollops of the ricotta mixture and the caramelised onions.
4. Launch the pizza into the oven and bake on a low flame, rotating the pizza 90 degrees every minute, for 4 minutes. Cook for a final minute with the flame on high to obtain a bit more colour, making sure to rotate the pizza frequently.
5. Once baked, place on a cooling screen or wire rack and rest for about 1 minute, then cut into 6–8 slices.
6. Finish with chopped parsley and shaved Pecorino Romano.

NY-style Pepperoni with Vodka Sauce

A fresh take on a NYC classic pepperoni. Rich and indulgent, with a sauce traditionally served with pasta.

Prep Time
10 mins

Cook Time
5 mins

Makes
1 x 14-inch pizza
(feeds 2-3 people)

100g (3.5oz) Vodka Sauce
  (page 86)
1 x 350g (12.3oz) New York-style
  Pizza dough ball (page 64)
100-125g (3.5-4.5oz) aged
  mozzarella, shredded
35-45g (1-1.6oz) fresh
  mozzarella, cut into 5 cubes
50g (1.8oz) pepperoni

To serve
Basil leaves
Pecorino Romano, grated
Extra virgin olive oil,
  for drizzling

1. Preheat your pizza oven to 340°C (650°F) (stone floor temperature).
2. Slowly heat the vodka sauce in a saucepan and leave over a low heat to keep warm.
3. Press and open the dough into a 14-inch circle and place on a lightly floured pizza peel.
4. Top the pizza with both mozzarellas first, then distribute the pepperoni over the top.
5. Launch the pizza into the oven and bake with a low flame, rotating the pizza 90 degrees every minute for 4 minutes. Cook for a final minute with the flame on high to obtain a bit more colour, making sure to rotate the pizza frequently.
6. Place the pizza on a cooling screen or wire rack and rest for 1 minute, then cut into 6–8 slices.
7. Once the pizza has been cut, use a ladle to drizzle the warm vodka sauce over the pizza.
8. Finish with basil, grated Pecorino Romano and drizzle with extra virgin olive oil.

Luis' NY-style Elotes Pizza

Luis Perez grew up in the Bronx before moving to upstate New York. He's gone from street pizza purveyor to a brick-n-mortar spot in Rochester. Blending New York-style pizza with Mexican-style street corn known as elotes, this combination speaks to his roots and his culinary journey, blending foods that represent who he is today.

Prep Time
20 mins

Cook Time
5 mins

Makes
1 x 14-inch pizza
(feeds 2-3 people)

---

1 x 350g (12.3oz) New York-style
  Pizza dough ball (page 64)
100-125g (3.5-4.5oz) aged
  mozzarella, shredded
35-45g (1-1.6oz) mild cheddar,
  cubed
1 corn cob, roasted and kernels
  removed (see corn recipe on
  page 231)
1 fresh jalapeño, sliced
100-125g (3.5-4.5oz) Mexican
  chorizo

For the crema
Bunch of coriander (cilantro)
255g (9oz) sour cream
85g (3oz) mayo
1 garlic clove
1 tsp salt
½ tsp freshly ground black pepper
1 tbsp lime juice

To serve
Dried chilli flakes
Cotija (aged Mexican cheese) or
  Pecorino Romano

1. **Preheat your pizza oven to 340°C (650°F) (stone floor temperature).**
2. **Blanch the coriander (cilantro) by immersing it in boiling water for 30–40 seconds, then transfer directly to a bowl of ice-cold water. Remove and dry.**
3. **Combine all the crema ingredients and blend until smooth using a food processor or immersion blender, then set to one side.**
4. **Press and open the dough into a 14-inch circle and place on a lightly floured peel.**
5. **Top the pizza with the shredded mozzarella followed by the cubed cheddar, then generously distribute the corn, jalapeño and chorizo over the top.**
6. **Launch the pizza into the oven and bake on a low flame, rotating the pizza 90 degrees every minute for 4 minutes. Cook for a final minute with the flame on high to obtain a bit more colour, making sure to rotate the pizza frequently.**
7. **Place on a cooling screen or wire rack and rest for 1 minute, then cut into 6–8 slices.**
8. **Finish with a drizzle of the crema, a pinch of chilli flakes and a scattering of finely grated cotija or Pecorino Romano.**

NY-style Sausage & Rapini Pizza

Rapini, aka broccoli rabe, brings a complex nutty and bitter flavour to this pizza. What better way to eat more greens?

Prep Time
30 mins

Cook Time
5 mins

Makes
1 x 14-inch pizza
(feeds 2-3 people)

100g (3.5oz) rapini or broccoli
1 x 350g (12.3oz) New York-style
  Pizza dough ball (page 64)
100-125g (3.5-4.5oz) aged
  mozzarella, shredded
35-45g (1-1.6oz) fresh
  mozzarella, cubed
50-75g (1.75-2.6oz) cooked fennel
  sausage
Pinch of flaky sea salt
Extra virgin olive oil,
  for drizzling

To serve
Pinch of dried oregano
Grated zest of $\frac{1}{2}$ lemon
Plenty of grated Pecorino Romano
Garlic Cream (page 97),
  for drizzling

1. Preheat your pizza oven to 340°C (650°F) (stone floor temperature).
2. Put the rapini or broccoli, some olive oil and a pinch of sea salt in a cast-iron pan and roast in the oven for a couple of minutes until wilted. Remove and set aside.
3. Press and open the dough into a 14-inch circle and place onto a lightly floured peel.
4. Top with the aged mozzarella, the fresh mozzarella and roasted rapini or broccoli, crumble over the sausage and drizzle with some olive oil.
5. Launch the pizza into the oven and bake on a low flame, rotating the pizza 90 degrees every minute for 4 minutes. Cook for a final minute with the flame on high to obtain a bit more colour, making sure to rotate the pizza frequently.
6. Once baked, place on a cooling screen or wire rack and rest for about 1 minute, then cut into 6-8 slices.
7. Top with oregano, lemon zest, Pecorino Romano and a drizzle of garlic cream and extra virgin olive oil.

Jhy's Italian Sausage & Hot Honey Pizza

Devoured Pop-Up's Jhy Coulter brings the culinary fervor of Kansas City to this take on a sausage pizza with a kick. Jhy built her business after winning a Roccbox on Instagram and is now a regular guest chef at Gozney HQ. From the street pizza pro herself, it's going to get hot.

Prep Time
1 hour

Cook Time
5 mins

Makes
1 x 14-inch pizza
(feeds 2-3 people)

---

2 shallots, thinly sliced
20g (0.7oz) unsalted butter
100ml (3.4fl oz) red wine
1 x 350g (12.3oz) New York-style
    Pizza dough ball (page 64)
230g (8.1oz) Simple Tomato Sauce
    (page 82)
226g (8oz) low-moisture mozzarella
7 Confit Garlic cloves (page 103)
Flaky sea salt and freshly ground
    black pepper

For the Italian sausage
113g (4oz) pork mince
A pinch of: fennel seeds, brown
    sugar, garlic powder, onion
    powder, dried parsley, dried
    basil, dried oregano, paprika,
    salt, dried chilli flakes
2 tsp red wine vinegar

To serve
Fresh herbs (parsley, thyme,
    rosemary)
Pecorino Romano, grated,
    Parmigiano Reggiano, Hot Honey,
    extra virgin olive oil
Garlic Oil (optional) (page 85)

1. Preheat your pizza oven to 340°C (650°F) (stone floor temperature).
2. Mix the Italian sausage ingredients together in a bowl, then cook in a hot cast-iron pan in the pizza oven, breaking the meat up as you cook it, until it's crumbled and crispy. (You will need to place it back in the oven for a few minutes to help crisp it up and cook through.)
3. Place a frying pan over a medium-high heat, then add the shallots, butter and red wine, along with some salt and pepper, and cook for about 15 minutes until the wine has reduced and the shallots have caramelised. Remove from the heat.
4. Press and open the dough into a 14-inch circle and place onto a lightly floured peel. Top the pizza with the tomato sauce, a layer of mozzarella, ground pork, caramelised shallots and tear the confit garlic cloves over the top.
5. Launch the pizza into the oven and bake on a low flame, rotating the pizza 90 degrees every minute for 4 minutes. Cook for a final minute with the flame on high to obtain a bit more colour, making sure to rotate the pizza frequently.
6. Place on a cooling screen or wire rack and rest for 1 minute, then cut into 6–8 slices.
7. Top with the fresh herbs, Pecorino Romano and Parmigiano Reggiano. Drizzle over the hot honey and olive oil and brush the crust with garlic oil to finish (if you like).

Detroit-style Red Top Pizza

The quintessential Detroit-style pizza. Thick with a crispy cheese crust, this mouth-watering pizza is not one to miss.

Prep Time
1 hour

Cook Time
15 mins

Makes
1 x 10 x 8-inch pizza
(feeds 4–6 people)

---

1 x 300g (10.5oz) Detroit-style
  Pan Pizza dough ball (page 68)
Olive oil, for greasing
150g (5.3oz) Marinara Sauce
  (page 84)
125g (4.4oz) mozzarella, shredded
125g (4.4oz) cheddar cheese,
  shredded

To serve
Plenty of grated Parmigiano
  Reggiano
Extra virgin olive oil,
  for drizzling

1. Using a cold dough ball, coat a 25 × 20cm (10 × 8in) pizza pan and the dough ball with a drizzle of oil, then dimple and pan-stretch the dough, working it towards the corners of the pan. Repeat this 4–5 times at 20-minute intervals (cover the pan between stretches with a lid or chopping board). As soon as the dough has reached and filled all four corners of the pan, cover and proof at room temperature until the dough has doubled in volume (time will vary based on the room temperature).
2. Preheat your pizza oven to 340°C (650°F) (stone floor temperature).
3. Heat the marinara sauce in a saucepan over a low heat, then keep it hot until needed.
4. With generously oiled fingertips, dimple the dough. Place the pan in the oven, turn the flame off and place the door on the oven. Par-bake for 2 minutes, then rotate the pizza 180 degrees, replace the door and bake for another 2 minutes. Remove and allow the dough to rest at room temperature. Turn the oven flame back on and heat the oven to 330°C (625°F).
5. Top the baked dough with the shredded cheese, ensuring generous and even coverage and spreading the cheese to the very edge of the pan. Launch the pan back into the oven and bake for 4 minutes with the door on and flame off, rotating the pizza 180 degrees after 2 minutes.
6. After 4 minutes, remove the door and turn the flame to high to obtain a bit more colour while rotating the pizza frequently until you reach your desired colour.
7. Once baked through, remove from the pan immediately with an offset spatula. Place on a cooling screen or wire rack and rest for about 1 minute, then cut into 4–6 pieces.
8. Top the pizza with the warm sauce and Parmigiano Reggiano.

Detroit-style Pepperoni Fire

A spicy take on our classic Detroit. This pizza packs flavour and is perfect if you love a little heat.

Prep Time
1 hour

Cook Time
15 mins

Makes
1 x 10 x 8-inch pizza
(feeds 4-6 people)

---

1 x 300g (10.5oz) Detroit-style
   Pan Pizza dough ball (page 68)
Olive oil, for greasing
150g (5.3oz) Marinara Sauce
   (page 84)
125g (4.4oz) mozzarella, shredded
125g (4.4oz) cheddar cheese,
   shredded
50g (1.8oz) sliced pepperoni
25g (0.9oz) red onion,
   thinly sliced

To serve

25g (0.9oz) Candied Jalapeño
   (page 105)
3 or 4 leaves of fresh basil,
   thinly cut
Plenty of grated Parmigiano
   Reggiano
Extra virgin olive oil
Hot Honey (page 89),
   for drizzling

1. Please refer to Step 1 Detroit-style Red Top recipe (page 153).
2. Preheat your pizza oven to 340°C (650°F) (stone floor temperature).
3. Heat the marinara sauce in a saucepan over a low heat and keep hot until needed.
4. With generously oiled fingertips, dimple the dough. Place the pan in the oven, turn the flame off and place the door on the oven. Par-bake for 2 minutes, then rotate the pizza 180 degrees, replace the door and bake for another 2 minutes. Remove and allow the dough to rest at room temperature. Turn the oven flame back on and heat the oven to 330°C (625°F).
5. Top the baked dough with both cheeses, ensuring generous and even coverage and spreading the cheese to the very edge of the pan. Add the pepperoni and the onion to the top of the pizza, launch the pan back into the oven and bake for 4 minutes with the door on and flame off, rotating the pizza 180 degrees after 2 minutes.
6. After 4 minutes, remove the door and turn the flame to high to obtain a bit more colour while rotating the pizza frequently.
7. Once baked, remove from the pan immediately with an offset spatula. Place on a cooling screen and rest for about 1 minute, then cut into 4-6 pieces. Top the pizza with candied jalapeño, warm marinara sauce, basil, Parmigiano Reggiano, drizzle with extra virgin olive oil and hot honey.

Detroit-style White Top Pizza

Topped with truffle oil, mushrooms and stracciatella, this is a rich, creamy, indulgent white Detroit-style pizza.

Prep Time
1 hour

Cook Time
15 mins

Makes
1 x 10 x 8-inch pizza
(feeds 4–6 people)

---

1 x 300g (10.5oz) Detroit-style
   Pan Pizza dough ball (page 68)
olive oil, for greasing
100g (3.5oz) mushrooms
   (ideally blue oyster), sliced
50g (1.8oz) Garlic in Oil
   (page 85), thinly sliced
125g (4.4oz) mozzarella, shredded
125g (4.4oz) cheddar cheese,
   shredded

To serve
A pinch of dried oregano
Small handful of roughly chopped
   flat-leaf parsley
Plenty of grated Pecorino Romano
100g (3.5oz) stracciatella
   di bufala
White truffle oil, for drizzling

1. Please refer to Step 1 Detroit-style Red Top recipe (page 153).
2. Preheat your pizza oven to 340°C (650°F) (stone floor temperature).
3. To roast the mushrooms, preheat a hot cast-iron pan in the oven, coat them with olive oil, season with sea salt and sear in the hot pan for 3–4 minutes, using a high flame. Set aside and leave to cool.
4. With generously oiled fingertips, dimple the dough. Place the pan in the oven, turn the flame off and place the door on the oven. Par-bake for 2 minutes, then rotate the pizza 180 degrees, replace the door and bake for another 2 minutes. Remove and allow the dough to rest at room temperature. Turn the oven flame back on and heat the oven to 330°C (625°F).
5. Top the baked dough with the garlic in oil and both cheeses, ensuring generous and even coverage and spreading the cheese to the very edge of the pan. Place the mushrooms on top of the cheese, launch the pan back into the oven and bake for 4 minutes with the door on and flame off, rotating the pizza 180 degrees after 2 minutes.
6. After 4 minutes, remove the door and turn the flame to high to obtain a bit more colour while rotating the pizza frequently.
7. Once baked, remove from the pan immediately with an offset spatula. Place onto a cooling screen or wire rack and rest for about 1 minute, then cut into 4–6 pieces.
8. Top the pizza with oregano, parsley, Pecorino Romano, stracciatella and a drizzle of truffle oil.

Detroit-style Trio Pizza

When one sauce just isn't enough. This pizza tastes just as good as it looks.

Prep Time
1 hour

Cook Time
15 mins

Makes
1 x 10 x 8-inch pizza
(feeds 4–6 people)

---

1 x 300g (10.5oz) Detroit-style
Pan Pizza dough ball (page 68)
Olive oil, for greasing
100g (3.5oz) Marinara Sauce
(page 84)
75g (2.6oz) Vodka Sauce (page 86)
125g (4.4oz) mozzarella, shredded
125g (4.4oz) cheddar cheese,
shredded
50g (1.8oz) Basil Pesto (page 94)
Plenty of Pecorino Romano, grated

1. Please refer to Step 1 Detroit-style Red Top recipe (page 153).
2. Preheat your pizza oven to 340°C (650°F) (stone floor temperature).
3. Heat the marinara sauce and vodka sauce in separate saucepans over a low heat and keep warm until needed.
4. With generously oiled fingertips, dimple the dough. Place the pan in the oven, turn the flame off and place the door on the oven. Par-bake for 2 minutes, then rotate the pizza 180 degrees, replace the door and bake for another 2 minutes. Remove and allow the dough to rest at room temperature. Turn the oven flame back on and heat the oven to 330°C (625°F).
5. Top the baked dough with the shredded cheese, ensuring generous and even coverage and spreading the cheese to the very edge of the pan. Launch the pan back into the oven and bake for 4 minutes with the door on and flame off, rotating the pizza 180 degrees after 2 minutes.
6. After 4 minutes, remove the door and turn the flame to high to obtain a bit more colour while rotating the pizza frequently.
7. Once baked, remove from the pan immediately with an offset spatula. Place onto a cooling screen or wire rack and rest for about 1 minute, then cut into 4–6 pieces.
8. Top the pizza with the sauces and pesto, alternating them diagonally or any way you fancy! Finish with Pecorino Romano.

Daniele's Roman-style Cacio e Pepe Pizza

In the heart of LA you can find restaurateur Daniele Uditi showing the US' West Coast what true Italian-inspired pizza is at his pizzeria, Pizzana. Simple and brilliant flavours from a renowned pizza purist.

Prep Time
10 mins

Cook Time
3 mins

Makes
1 x 12-inch pizza
(feeds 1–2 people)

250g (8.8oz) whole-milk ricotta

50g (1.8oz) Parmigiano Reggiano, grated

150g (5.3oz) Pecorino Romano, grated

50g (1.8oz) panna da cucina or double (heavy) cream

1 x 180g (6.3oz) Roman-style Pizza dough ball (page 70)

90g (3.1oz) fior di latte mozzarella

Extra virgin olive oil, for drizzling

Flaky sea salt and freshly ground black pepper

1. Preheat your pizza oven to 385°C (725°F) (stone floor temperature).
2. Combine the ricotta with the Parmigiano Reggiano, half the Pecorino Romano and half the panna da cucina in a bowl.
3. In a separate bowl, make the base sauce by combining the remaining panna da cucina with some salt and black pepper to taste.
4. Press and open the dough into a 12-inch circle, pushing the air with your fingers from the outside of the circle to the inside. Top with the base sauce, the other half of the grated Pecorino Romano and hand-torn chunks of the fior di latte.
5. Transfer to a lightly floured peel and redistribute any toppings as required.
6. Launch the pizza into the oven and bake on a high flame for 45 seconds, then rotate the pizza 90 degrees every 10–15 seconds until crispy and charred.
7. Once baked, slice and add a spoon of your ricotta mixture to each slice. Finish with black pepper, olive oil and a pinch of sea salt flakes.

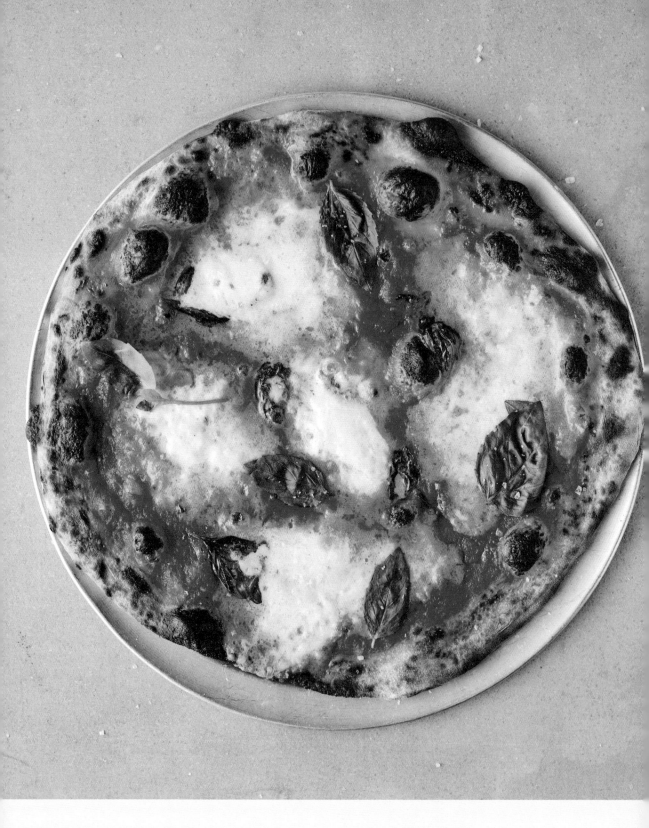

Roman-style Margherita

A classic Margherita Roman-style with fresh Buffalo Mozzarella. For those that like their pizzas thin and crispy.

Prep Time
10 mins

Cook Time
3 mins

Makes
1 x 12-inch pizza
(feeds 1-2 people)

---

1 x 180g (6.3oz) Roman-style
  Pizza dough ball (page 70)
120g (4.2oz) Simple Tomato Sauce
  (page 82)
Pecorino or Parmigiano Reggiano,
  grated
A few fresh basil leaves, torn
80g (2.8oz) fior di latte
  mozzarella
Extra virgin olive oil, for
  drizzling

1. Preheat your pizza oven to 385°C (725°F) (stone floor temperature).
2. Press and open the dough into a 12-inch circle, pushing the air with your fingers from the outside of the circle to the inside.
3. Top the pizza with the tomato sauce, grated pecorino or Parmigiano Reggiano, some of the basil leaves and hand-torn chunks of the fior di latte.
4. Transfer to a lightly floured peel and redistribute any toppings as required.
5. Drizzle over some olive oil and launch the pizza into the oven and bake on a high flame for 45 seconds, then rotate the pizza 90 degrees every 10 seconds until crispy and charred.
6. Once baked, finish with more basil leaves and olive oil.

Roman-style Potato & Rosemary Pizza

A classic Italian flavour pairing. This is an earthy and aromatic pizza with super thin and crisp slices of potato and a classic Roman-style crust.

Prep Time
10 mins

Cook Time
3 mins

Makes
1 x 12 x 8-inch pizza
(feeds 1-2 people)

150g (3oz) medium Yukon Gold
  potatoes, thinly sliced
  (unpeeled)
1 x 180g (6.3oz) Roman-style
  Pizza dough ball (page 70)
1-2 garlic cloves, thinly sliced
  and coated with oil
Extra virgin olive oil,
  for drizzling

To serve
Needles from 2 sprigs of rosemary
Plenty of Pecorino Romano, grated
Freshly ground black pepper

1. Soak the potato slices in cold salted water for at least 30 minutes and preheat your pizza oven to 385°C (725°F) (stone floor temperature).
2. Press and open the dough into a long and thin rectangle about 30 × 20cm (12 × 8in), without leaving space for a crust. Top evenly with the oiled sliced garlic. Layer on the sliced potatoes.
3. Transfer to a lightly floured peel and redistribute any toppings as required.
4. Drizzle over some olive oil, launch the pizza into the oven and bake on a high flame, rotating the pizza 90 degrees every 10 seconds, until crispy and charred.
5. Top with rosemary, plenty of grated Pecorino Romano and some cracked black pepper.

Roman-style Burrata, Rocket & Mortadella Pizza

This pizza is incredibly light and fresh. The burrata, rocket and mortadella are added post-bake making it the perfect pizza for a long, hot summer's day.

Prep Time
10 mins

Cook Time
3 mins

Makes
1 x 12 x 8-inch pizza
(feeds 1-2 people)

---

1 x 180g (6.3oz) Roman-style
   Pizza dough ball (page 70)
Extra virgin olive oil

To serve
60g (2.2oz) rocket (arugula)
90g (3oz) mortadella, thinly
   sliced
80g (2.8oz) burrata
Plenty of Pecorino Romano, grated

1. Preheat your pizza oven to 385°C (725°F) (stone floor temperature).
2. Press and open the dough into a long and thin rectangle about 30 × 20cm (12 × 8in), without leaving space for a crust. Perforate the dough all over with a fork and drizzle it with olive oil.
3. Transfer to a lightly floured peel, launch the pizza into the oven and bake on a high flame, rotating the pizza 90 degrees every 10 seconds until golden and charred.
4. Let the cooked base rest for 1 minute, then top with the rocket (arugula), mortadella and burrata. Finish with grated Pecorino Romano and extra virgin olive oil.

Tomato Pie

A pan pizza with tomatoes, garlic, oregano and olive oil, topped with breadcrumbs and Pecorino Romano. Saucy, crunchy and fresh.

Prep Time
1 hour

Cook Time
15 mins

Makes
1 x 10 x 10-inch pizza
(feeds 4-6 people)

---

1 x 450g (16oz) Sicilian style
   Pan Pizza dough ball (page 68)
Drizzle of olive or canola oil
100-125g (3.5-4.5oz) Simple
   Tomato Sauce (page 82)
25g (0.9oz) Confit Garlic
   (page 103), chopped
Olive oil, for greasing

To serve
Pinch of dried oregano
25g (0.9oz) toasted breadcrumbs
Plenty of grated Pecorino Romano
Extra virgin olive oil,
   for drizzling

1. Lightly grease a 25cm (10in), 5cm (2in) deep pan with olive oil. Place in a cold dough ball, drizzle with oil and then stretch it towards the corners of the pan and dimple. Repeat this about 4–5 times at 20-minute intervals (cover the pan between stretches with a lid or chopping board). As soon as the dough has reached and filled all four corners of the pan, cover and proof at room temperature until the dough has doubled in volume (time will vary based on the room temperature).

2. Preheat your pizza oven to 330°C (625°F) (stone floor temperature).

3. With generously oiled fingertips, dimple the dough. Place the pan in the oven, turn the flame off and place the door on the oven. Par-bake for 2 minutes, then rotate the pizza 180 degrees, replace the door and bake for another 2 minutes. Remove and allow the dough to rest at room temperature. Turn the oven flame back on and heat the oven to 330°C (625°F).

4. Remove the par-cooked dough from the pan, coat the pan and outer crust lightly with oil and place the dough back in the pan. Top with the tomato sauce and chopped confit garlic, place the pan back into the oven and bake for 4 minutes with the door on and flame off, rotating the pizza 180 degrees after 2 minutes.

5. After 4 minutes, remove the door and turn the flame to high while rotating frequently for 30 seconds to obtain a bit more colour.

6. Remove the pizza from the pan immediately and place on a cooling screen or wire rack to rest for 1 minute, then cut into 4–6 pieces.

7. Top the pizza with oregano, breadcrumbs, Pecorino Romano and a generous amount olive oil.

Sicilian-style Cheese Pizza

A pan version of a classic Margherita with a light, airy and crispy fired underside. Once you've tried this, you'll be making it time and time again.

Prep Time
10 mins

Cook Time
8–10 mins

Makes
1 x 10 x 10-inch pizza
(feeds 4–6 people)

---

1 x 450g (15.5oz) Sicilian-style
  Pan Pizza dough ball (page 68)
1 tsp olive or canola oil
125–150g (4.5–5.5oz) aged
  mozzarella, sliced
100–125g (3.5–4.5oz) Simple
  Tomato Sauce (page 82)
35–45g (1–1.6oz) fresh mozzarella,
  cut into 5cm (2in) cubes

To serve
Fresh basil
Dried oregano
Grated Parmigiano Reggiano
Extra virgin olive oil,
  for drizzling

1. Lightly grease a 25cm (10in), 5cm (2in) deep pan with olive oil. Place in a cold dough ball, drizzle with oil and then stretch it towards the corners of the pan and dimple. Repeat this 4–5 times at 20-minute intervals (cover the pan between stretches with a lid or chopping board). As soon as the dough has reached and filled all four corners of the pan, cover and proof at room temperature until the dough has doubled in volume (time will vary based on the room temperature).

2. Preheat your pizza oven to 330°C (625°F) (stone floor temperature).

3. With generously oiled fingertips, dimple the dough. Place the pan in the oven, turn the flame off and place the door on the oven. Par-bake for 2 minutes, then rotate the pizza 180 degrees, replace the door and bake for another 2 minutes. Remove and allow the dough to rest at room temperature. Turn the oven flame back on and heat the oven to 330°C (625°F).

4. Remove the par-cooked dough from the pan, coat the pan and outer crust lightly with oil and place the dough back in the pan. Top with the sliced mozzarella, 3 stripes of tomato sauce and 5 cubes of fresh mozzarella on top of the sauce (1 cube in the centre and 1 at each corner). Launch the pan back into the oven and bake for 4 minutes with the door on and flame off, rotating the pizza 180 degrees after 2 minutes.

5. After 4 minutes, remove the door and turn the flame to high while rotating frequently for 30 seconds to obtain a bit more colour.

6. Once baked, remove from the pan immediately with an offset spatula and rest for 1 minute on a cooling screen or wire rack, then cut into 4–6 pieces. Top with basil, oregano, Parmigiano Reggiano and finish with a drizzle of olive oil.

Sesame Focaccia

This tear-and-share focaccia is perfect for cutting up to serve at parties, turning into sandwiches or simply serving with olive oil and balsamic. The sesame seeds add an amazing flavour and texture.

Prep Time
10 mins

Cook Time
8–10 mins

Makes
1 x 12 x 10-inch focaccia
(feeds 4-6 people)

---

1 tsp extra virgin olive oil,
  plus extra for drizzling
2 tbsp sesame seeds
1 x 550g (19.4oz) Focaccia dough
  ball (page 72)
Flaky sea salt

1. Lightly grease a 30 × 25cm (12 × 10in) pizza pan with olive oil, then coat the pan with sesame seeds. Place the dough ball into the pan and coat it with olive oil, then dimple and pan-stretch the dough, working it towards the corners of the pan. Repeat this 4–5 times at 20-minute intervals (cover the pan between stretches with a lid or chopping board). As soon as the dough has reached and filled all four corners of the pan, cover and proof at room temperature until the dough has doubled in volume (time will vary based on the room temperature).

2. Preheat your pizza oven to 315°C (600°F) (stone floor temperature).

3. With generously oiled fingertips, dimple the dough. Place the pan in the oven, turn the flame off and place the door onto the oven, bake for 3 minutes, then rotate the focaccia 180 degrees, replace the door and bake for another 3 minutes.

4. Remove the door, turn the flame on to low and bake for a further 1–2 minutes while rotating the focaccia frequently, until golden brown with some charring.

5. Once baked, remove the focaccia from the pan immediately and rest for 1 minute before drizzling it with more oil and sprinkling with flaky sea salt.

Tomato & Confit Garlic Focaccia

Taking the focaccia up a notch, the confit garlic and tomato add an incredible umami flavour. Experiment with your own toppings – anything goes.

Prep Time
45 mins

Cook Time
8–10 mins

Makes
1 x 12 x 10-inch focaccia
(feeds 4-6 people)

Extra virgin olive oil,
    for drizzling
1 x 550g (19.4oz) Focaccia dough
    ball (page 72)
9 Confit Garlic cloves (page 103)
16 Confit Tomatoes (page 104)

To serve
Flaky sea salt
A few fresh oregano leaves

1. Lightly grease a 30 × 25cm (12 × 10in) pizza pan with olive oil. Place the dough ball into the pan and coat with olive oil, then dimple and pan-stretch the dough, working it towards the corners of the pan. Repeat this 4–5 times at 20-minute intervals (cover the pan between stretches with a lid or chopping board). As soon as the dough has reached and filled all four corners of the pan, cover and proof at room temperature until the dough has doubled in volume (time will vary based on the room temperature).

2. Preheat your pizza oven to 330°C (625°F) (stone floor temperature).

3. With generously oiled fingertips, dimple the dough, then place the garlic cloves and tomatoes evenly across the surface, being sure to gently press them into the recesses of focaccia dough.

4. Place the pan in the oven, turn the flame off and place the door on the oven. Par-bake for 3 minutes, then rotate the focaccia 180 degrees and bake for another 3 minutes, again with the door on.

5. Remove the door, turn the flame to low and bake for a further 1–2 minutes, while rotating the focaccia frequently, until golden brown with some charring.

6. Remove the focaccia from the pan immediately and rest 1 minute before drizzling with olive oil and sprinkling with flaky salt and oregano leaves.

Focaccia Sandwich

Filled with Italian classics – prosciutto, mozzarella, rocket (arugula) – and drizzled with balsamic glaze, it doesn't get much better than this.

Prep Time
5 mins

―――――――――――――

$\frac{1}{6}$ of a focaccia (page 176)
75g (2.6oz) prosciutto
60g (2.1oz) mozzarella
Handful of rocket (arugula)
Balsamic glaze, for drizzling

Makes
1 sandwich using $\frac{1}{6}$ of a focaccia (page 176)

1. **This couldn't be easier. Simply slice the focaccia in half, then pile in the prosciutto, mozzarella and rocket (arugula) and drizzle over some balsamic glaze before serving.**

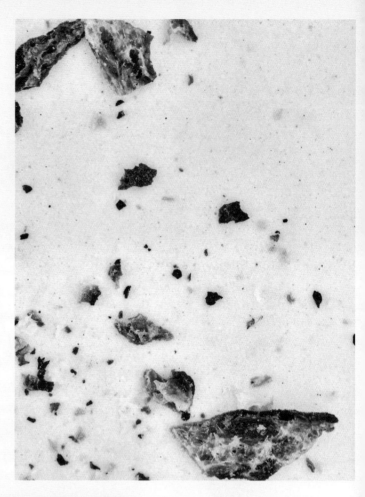

Neapolitan-style Calzone

Brimming with a saucy mix of Napoli salami, basil, fior di latte and ricotta, this mouth-watering calzone is a great alternative to a classic pizza.

Prep Time
10 mins

Cook Time
3-4 mins

Makes
1 x calzone pizza
(feeds 1-2 people)

260g (9.2oz) Neapolitan-style
  Pizza dough ball (page 60)
60g (2.1oz) ricotta
20g (0.7oz) sliced Napoli salami
40g (1.4oz) fior di latte
  mozzarella
2-3 basil leaves for inside
30g (1oz) Simple Tomato Sauce
  (page 82)
20g (0.7oz) Pecorino Romano, plus
  a little extra grated to garnish

To serve
Extra virgin olive oil
Fresh torn basil leaves

1. Preheat your pizza oven to 400°C (750°F) (stone floor temperature).
2. Open the dough out to a 10-inch circle and spoon the ricotta onto one half of the dough, making sure to leave a space around the edge to help you seal the calzone. Add the salami onto the ricotta and top with the fior di latte and basil leaves. Fold the empty side of the dough over the filled side to form a half-circle shape, then fully seal the crusts.
3. Once fully sealed, make sure it's not stuck to the surface by lifting and moving it about slightly (use some flour on the work surface if needed) and pinch a small hole in the middle top of the calzone to stop it from ballooning up in the oven.
4. Spread the tomato sauce carefully over the top, grate on the Pecorino and drizzle over some oil.
5. Launch the calzone into the oven and bake for 3-4 minutes, turning frequently to bake the dough and the filling.
6. Finish with a little extra grated Pecorino Romano, some fresh torn basil and a drizzle of olive oil.

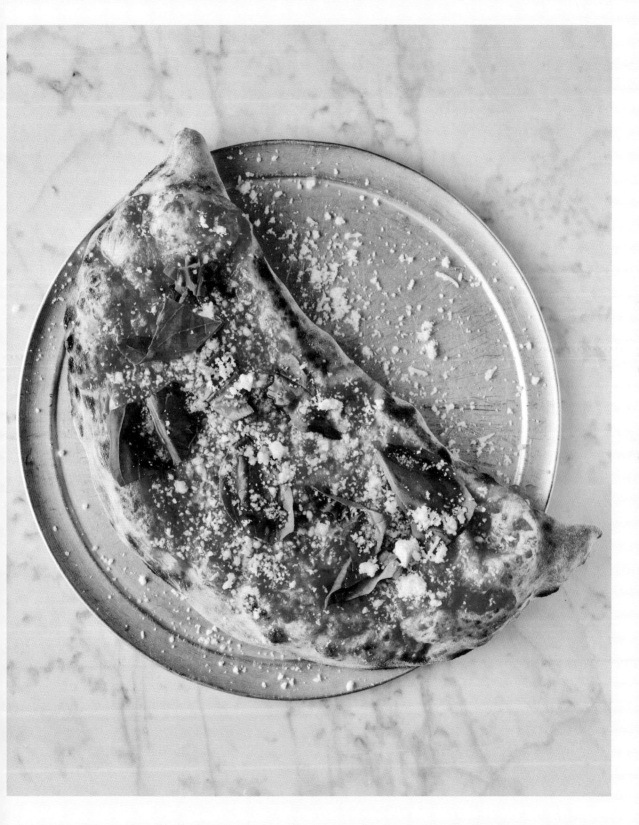

Chris' Chopped Cheese Calzone

Bold style you can't mess with, just like the Flamebaster himself, Chris Roberts. Inspired by the New York classic, the globe-hopping Welshman brings the world's flavours together in a hearty, savoury take on a calzone.

Prep Time
1 hour

Cook Time
3-4 mins

Makes
3 x calzone pizzas
(feeds 3-6 people)

---

1 large green (bell) pepper
3 beef burger patties
   (10-15% fat content)
100ml (3.4fl oz) beef stock
1 tbsp Worcestershire sauce
100g (3.5oz) gruyère, grated
100g (3.5oz) sharp cheddar,
   grated
100g (3.5oz) mozzarella or
   provolone, grated
3 x 260g (9.2oz) Neapolitan-style
   Pizza dough balls (page 60)
400g (14oz) Simple Tomato Sauce
   (page 82)
9 x American cheese slices
Flaky sea salt and ground white
   pepper

To serve
1 large white onion, diced
Large gherkins
Burger sauce

1. Preheat your pizza oven to 400°C (750°F) stone floor temperature.
2. Place the pepper directly on the oven floor for a few minutes so the skin catches and chars. Thinly slice the pepper, leaving the skin on but discarding the seeds, and set it to one side.
3. Heat a cast-iron pan over a high heat, then add the burger patties and fry for a few minutes on each side until they become nicely caramelised. You want some nice char here, so take it to the limit. (You may need to add a splash of oil if your meat has a lower percentage of fat.) Use a metal spatula to roughly chop the patties up into a crumble consistency, then add a good pinch of salt and pepper (white pepper is preferable here) or add a tablespoon of your favourite spice mix. Add the sliced pepper, then continue cooking and chopping until the beef is cooked and no longer pink. Deglaze the pan with the beef stock and Worcestershire sauce, then add the grated cheeses and continue to chop and stir until everything is well mixed. Taste and add extra seasoning if needed, then leave to cool to room temperature.
4. Stretch the dough out to a 10-inch circle and add a ladleful of tomato sauce to one half of the dough and add the cooled chopped cheese filling on top.
5. Lay the American cheese slices on top, then fold over and seal the calzone. Take your time with this to make sure none of the cheese leaks out!
6. Lightly flour your peel before transferring the calzone to the oven to cook for 2–3 minutes, turning them frequently, until the dough has risen and is golden brown in colour.
7. Serve with diced raw white onion, big gherkins, some burger sauce and plenty of napkins.

07 Outdoor

A pizza oven is for more than just pizza. There are limitless possibilities of what you can cook with fire and the high temperatures pizza ovens reach.

For Tom, nights spent cooking and tending the fire while connecting with friends and loved ones was a life-changing turning point. He discovered how cooking with fire brings people together.

We've gathered some of our favourite non-pizza recipes to cook outdoors for you to create and share with others.

Sea Salt Steak

You haven't had the best steak of your life until you've cooked with the high temperature of a pizza oven. Tender meat on the inside and crusted bark on the outside. This is the stuff of neighbourhood outdoor cooking heroes.

Prep Time
30 mins

Cook Time
7 mins, plus
resting time

Serves
1 or 2

---

1 thick-cut bone-in rib-eye steak
Olive oil, for rubbing
30g (1oz) unsalted butter
Flaky sea salt and freshly ground
    black pepper

1. **Preheat your pizza oven to 400°C (750°F) (stone floor temperature).**
2. **While the oven is heating up, bring the steak to room temperature for at least 30 minutes. Pat it dry with kitchen paper before rubbing it with a little oil and seasoning generously with flaky sea salt.**
3. **Place a cast-iron pan in the oven for a few minutes to get very hot. Remove the pan from the oven and place the steak in, fat side down, holding it in place with tongs. Cook for 30 seconds or so, then lay the steak flat and place the pan back in the oven for about 6 minutes, turning the steak halfway through.**
4. **Add the butter and cook for a few more minutes, basting it every now and then outside of the oven and being careful not to let the butter burn. Continue to cook until the steak reaches an internal temperature of 52°C (125°F) for medium rare or 62°C (143°F) for medium – test it using a temperature probe.**
5. **Place the steak on a plate, pour over the cooking juices, season generously with freshly ground black pepper and leave to rest for 10 minutes. During this time, the internal temperature of the steak will increase by a few degrees.**
6. **Slice and serve with the juices and a final sprinkling of flaky sea salt.**

Dukkah Lamb Cutlets

Succulent lamb cutlets topped with the nuttiness and earthiness of dukkah. A perfect sharing dish to be enjoyed with the whole family.

Prep Time
10 mins

Cook Time
10 mins

Serves
4

---

2 tbsp olive oil

Grated zest of 1 lemon

8 lamb cutlets

60g (2.1oz) feta, crumbled

60g (2.1oz) pomegranate seeds

Handful of mint leaves

Handful of coriander (cilantro)
    leaves

For the dukkah

70g (2.5oz) blanched hazelnuts

40g (1.4oz) shelled and unsalted
    pistachios

40g (1.4oz) white sesame seeds

$\frac{1}{4}$ tsp fennel seeds

1 tsp coriander seeds

1 tsp cumin seeds

1 tsp flaky sea salt

1. Prepare the dukkah by toasting the hazelnuts and pistachios in a large frying pan over a medium-high heat for a few minutes, then adding the remaining ingredients and toasting for about 2–3 more minutes until fragrant. Leave the mix to cool, then pulse in a food processor until finely chopped but still with some texture. Remove all but 3 tablespoons of the dukkah from the processor, then blend the remaining mixture into a fine powder. (Any leftover dukkah will keep in an airtight jar for up to 3 weeks.)

2. Mix the fine dukkah in a bowl with the olive oil and the lemon zest, then add the lamb to the bowl and toss together until well coated.

3. Preheat your pizza oven to 250°C (480°F) (stone floor temperature) with a low flame and place a cast-iron pan in the oven for about 10 minutes to get searingly hot.

4. Place the cutlets in the pan and cook in the oven for 2 minutes before turning them over and cooking for 2 more minutes. Take the pan out of the oven and stand the chops up on the fat cap and leave for about a minute so the fat can render a little.

5. Place the lamb on a board to rest for 5 minutes, then serve on a platter with the feta, pomegranate, herbs and a few tablespoons of the dukkah scattered over the top. Cut the zested lemon into wedges and serve alongside.

Meatballs

Smoky, tender meatballs hugged by a rich, flavoursome tomato sauce. A crowd-pleaser that is truly versatile and works great with pasta, as a pizza topping or as a standalone.

Prep Time	Cook Time	Serves
15 mins	10 mins	4

---

1 tbsp fennel seeds

½ tsp dried chilli flakes

½ tsp dried oregano

1 tsp chopped fresh sage

1 tbsp chopped fresh rosemary

250g (8.8oz) pork mince

250g (8.8oz) veal mince

2 tbsp breadcrumbs

30g (1oz) Parmigiano Reggiano, grated, plus extra to serve

2 tsp Dijon mustard

1 egg

1 tbsp olive oil

300g (10.5oz) Simple Tomato Sauce (page 82)

Flaky sea salt and freshly ground black pepper

1. Preheat your pizza oven to 400°C (750°F) (stone floor temperature).
2. Use a pestle and mortar to grind the fennel seeds, chilli flakes, dried oregano, chopped sage and chopped rosemary together, then mix with the pork and veal mince in a large bowl. Add the breadcrumbs, grated Parmigiano Reggiano, mustard and egg and a good pinch each of salt and pepper.
3. Divide the mix into 25g (0.9oz) meatballs and set to one side.
4. Heat a cast-iron pan in the oven for a few minutes, then add the oil and the meatballs and cook for 5–6 minutes, shaking the pan regularly.
5. Spoon the tomato sauce over the meatballs, swirl the pan to emulsify the fat into the sauce and place back in the oven for 2–3 minutes. Remove the meatballs from the oven and grate over a generous amount of Parmigiano Reggiano before serving.

Jon & Vinny's Skirt Steak

Jon Shook and Vinny Dotolo, the chefs and creators behind Los Angeles' ground-breaking restaurants like Jon & Vinny's and Son of a Gun, give you a peek behind their culinary curtain with this signature steak recipe. A regular backyard favourite for both, and a standout on the menu at Jon & Vinny's.

Prep Time
24 hours

Cook Time
10 mins

Serves
4

---

1 x 750ml (25fl oz) bottle
  Italian red wine (Montepulciano)
100g (3.5oz) granulated sugar
6 cloves
Pinch of freshly grated nutmeg
1 cinnamon stick
Pared peel from 1 orange,
  cut into large strips
4 x 225g (8oz) skirt steaks
Neutral oil, for drizzling
Extra virgin olive oil,
  for drizzling
Kosher salt, to taste
Freshly ground black pepper
Thick slices of red onion, pan-
  fried until charred, to serve

1. Place the red wine, sugar, cloves, nutmeg, cinnamon stick and orange zest in a saucepan and bring to a rolling boil before turning the heat down and simmering for 15 minutes.
2. Next, take the pan off the heat and leave the marinade to cool (you can speed this up by placing the pan in an ice bath), then remove and discard the aromatics.
3. Add the steak to the marinade and leave in the fridge for 24 hours (48 at the most).
4. When you're ready to cook, heat your pizza oven to its highest temperature about 450°C (850°F) (stone floor temperature). Remove your steak from the marinade, pat it dry and leave it to come to room temperature before seasoning with salt and pepper.
5. Put a large cast-iron pan in the oven to preheat for 5 minutes, then add a splash of neutral oil. Add the steaks to the pan and sear the first side for 1–2 minutes before flipping and cooking for a few minutes more. You want a nice hot pan to make sure you get some caramelisation on the outside.
6. Cook to your liking, then leave to rest for 5 minutes before slicing. Serve with a drizzle of extra virgin olive oil, some flaky salt and some grilled red onion slices if you'd like.

Wood-fired Chicken & Onion Flatbread

The beauty of this wood-fired recipe lies with the roasting of the chicken. A bed of onions soak up all the juices, giving them extra flavour, while also keeping the chicken moist and succulent.

Prep Time
15 mins

Cook Time
1 hour

Serves
4

---

1 chicken (about 1.5kg/3.3lb)
4 large white onions, cut into
   1cm (0.3in)-thick slices
80ml (2.7fl oz) olive oil
1 x 350g (12.3oz) Signature-style
   Pizza dough ball (page 58)
Small handful of parsley, chopped
Flaky sea salt and freshly ground
   black pepper

1. Build a wood fire in your pizza oven and let it burn down to embers.
2. While the fire is burning, spatchcock the chicken by using poultry shears or a sharp knife to remove its backbone, then turn it breast side up and press down hard to lay the chicken flat.
3. Lay the sliced onions in the bottom of a roasting tray and sit the chicken on top, breast side up. Drizzle the oil over the chicken and onions, then season generously with salt and pepper.
4. When the fire has burnt to embers and your oven's stone floor temperature is at about 200°C (390°F), place the tray in the oven with the legs closest to the embers and put the door on with the vents closed. If cooking with gas, turn off the oven completely and then put the door on with the vents closed. (Never use the oven with the door on when using gas.) Cook for 40–50 minutes, turning the roasting tray three or four times, until the chicken is crispy and golden and it reaches an internal temperature of 75°C (168°F) at its thickest part.
5. Cover and leave the chicken to rest.
6. Now it's time for the flatbread. Add a couple of pieces of wood to the embers to bring the oven up to 450°C (850°F).
7. Once the oven is up to temperature, roll out the dough into a large rectangle approximately 30cm (14-inch) in length and transfer to a light-floured peel. Carefully launch the dough into the oven and bake for a minute or so, turning it regularly, until golden, crispy and charred to your liking.
8. Serve the flatbread on a large serving plate and top with the onions and the whole chicken so all the oil and juices soak into the flatbread. Sprinkle with some flaky salt and parsley, then serve.

Tips

If your chicken is getting a little crispier and more golden than you were going for, but it's still not fully cooked through, just use a little foil to cover it.

Cedar Plank Salmon

Plank cooking is a fun and sensory way to cook. The charred cedar plank infuses the salmon with a smoky flavour to make the best salmon we've ever had.

Prep Time
10 mins, plus soaking time

Cook Time
10-15 mins

Serves
3-4

---

1 side of salmon (about 500g/ 17.6oz), skin on, pin bones removed
1 tbsp olive oil
1 untreated food safe cedar plank, soaked in water for 6-8 hours
Flaky sea salt

1. Firstly, ensure your salmon is a suitable size for the plank by trimming off near the tail and belly. These bits can be saved for another meal.
2. Rub the salmon with the olive oil, then season generously with flaky salt.
3. Preheat your pizza oven to 350°C (660°F) (stone floor temperature), using gas or wood and ensuring you have a medium/medium-high flame.
4. Remove the plank from its soaking water and lay the fish, skin side down on the wood. Slide the plank into the centre of the oven. Cook the salmon for 10-15 minutes until it reaches an internal temperature of 51°C (125°F) for a medium cook, adding a little more time if you'd like it cooked further, and use a pizza peel and/or tongs to turn and rotate the plank during the cooking time.

Roasted Sea Bream with Olive & Herb Dressing

There's something so special about roasting fish at a high heat, giving you crispy skin and tons of flavour, paired with a green olive and herb dressing. You can replace the bream with sea bass if you want.

Prep Time
5 mins

Cook Time
10–15 mins

Serves
4

---

2 whole sea bream (about 500g/
   17.6oz each), scaled and
   gutted
1 lemon
Sea salt and freshly ground black
   pepper
Olive oil, for drizzling

For the dressing
30g (1oz) pitted green olives,
   roughly chopped
1 tbsp capers, roughly chopped
Small bunch of parsley,
   roughly chopped
Grated zest of 1 lemon
Extra virgin olive oil,
   for drizzling

1. Preheat your pizza oven to 250°C (480°F) (stone floor temperature) and heat a baking tray in the oven for a few minutes.
2. To make the dressing, mix together the olives, capers and parsley in a bowl, then stir in the grated lemon zest. Add the juice from half the zested lemon, along with a small glug of olive oil and season to taste.
3. Make 3 shallow diagonal cuts on each side of the fish, rub a little olive oil all over both the sea bream and season generously with salt and pepper. Slice the lemon and place the slices in the fish cavities. Place on the preheated baking tray and roast in the oven for 10–15 minutes, until the fish is cooked through, then top with the dressing and serve.

Brad's Roasted Oysters with Fermented Chilli

Chef and giant personality, Brad Leone, knows his way around foraging, harvesting and fermenting. He also loves an oyster, especially one plucked from the coastal waters of New England. His recipe changes things up with a little heat, yet still keeps it fresh and light.

Prep Time
5 mins, plus 2 weeks fermenting time

Cook Time
5 mins

Serves
3-4

---

12 fresh oysters
100g (3.5oz) unsalted butter
A few sprigs of rosemary,
   needles stripped
A few sage leaves

For the fermented chilli paste
907g (32oz) fresh chillies, e.g.,
   cayenne, scotch bonnet,
   jalapeño (use your favourites)
2 lemongrass stalks
1 head of garlic, cloves
   separated and peeled
5cm (2in) piece of ginger
240ml (8fl oz) shoyu
Fine sea salt (weight variable)

1. Weigh all of the ingredients for the fermented chilli, then add half of that weight in fine sea salt. Blitz the mixture in a food processor until you have a thick paste, then place in a sterilised airtight jar and leave for 2 weeks at room temperature.
2. Strain off the liquid after 2 weeks, then pack the paste into clean jars and store in the fridge for up to 2 months.
3. Preheat your pizza oven to 430°C (800°F) (stone floor temperature) and lay out the oysters on a roasting tray, then cook in the oven for 5 minutes. (You can nestle the oysters in some flaky salt to help them sit flat and to look great ready for serving!)
4. Create a herby butter by heating the unsalted butter in a small saucepan with a spoon of the fermented chilli paste and some rosemary needles and sage leaves. Be careful not to burn the butter.
5. Remove the oysters from the oven, open and serve with the fermented chilli butter.

Seafood Bake

This quick and easy seafood bake features mussels, prawns, clams, andouille, potatoes and sweetcorn in a buttery sauce.

Prep Time
20 mins

Cook Time
10 mins

Serves
2

600g (21.2oz) mixed shellfish,
   e.g., mussels, prawns, clams,
   crawfish
2 tbsp olive oil
3 tbsp Old Bay seasoning
2 garlic cloves, minced
2 tsp Cajun seasoning
200g (7oz) small potatoes, boiled
2 corn cobs, halved and boiled
2 andouille sausages or kielbasa,
   cut into big chunks
2 lemons, halved
Flaky sea salt and freshly ground
   black pepper

For the garlic butter
60g (2.1oz) unsalted butter
2 garlic cloves, finely chopped
Small bunch of parsley,
   finely chopped

1. Preheat your pizza oven to 250°C (480°F) stone floor temperature with a medium flame.
2. Clean the shellfish and pull the beards off the mussels. Discard any mussels and clams that are broken or don't close when tapped on the work surface.
3. In a small bowl combine the oil, Old Bay seasoning, garlic and Cajun seasoning along with some salt and pepper.
4. Spread the shellfish, potatoes, corn and sausage chunks onto a large baking tray and mix together with the spiced oil. Nestle the lemon halves in and cook in the oven for about 10 minutes, turning the tray a few times and tossing the ingredients around, until the prawns are a beautiful pink colour, the clams and mussels have all opened up and the sausages are cooked through.
5. Put the butter and garlic in a small saucepan and place just inside the oven so the butter melts, then stir through the parsley.
6. Drizzle the garlic butter over the seafood and squeeze over the roasted lemon halves.

Lee's Clams, Bacon & Mussels

Long-time friend, OG Gozney supporter and culinary mastermind Lee Tiernan brings his progressive London, rock 'n' roll approach to delicious food. Complex flavours put together with elegant simplicity, like a 4-chord anthem. Try his take on mussels and clams – amplified with bacon.

Prep Time	Cook Time	Serves
15 mins	10 mins	4–6

---

1 tbsp neutral oil

300g (10.5oz) smoked bacon lardons

2 red chillies, thinly sliced

4 garlic cloves, thinly sliced

3 spring onions (scallions), sliced

50g (1.8oz) ginger, cut into matchsticks

300g (10.5oz) mussels, scrubbed clean and debearded

300g (10.5oz) clams or cockles

250ml (8.5fl oz) cider, white wine or vermouth (or whatever you fancy, such as sherry, beer or flat champagne)

50g (1.8oz) butter, cut into small chunks

Handful of coriander (cilantro) leaves

Handful of Thai basil leaves

Large handful of spinach

1 lime, cut into wedges

1. Preheat your pizza oven to 250°C (480°F) (stone floor temperature) and place a very large frying pan or paella pan in the oven to heat up.

2. When the pan is just starting to smoke, add the oil, then add the bacon lardons and place the pan back into the oven, stirring them every so often until crispy and golden.

3. Add the chilli, garlic, spring onion and ginger, cook for a minute or two, then toss in the mussels and choice of clams or cockles. Carefully pour in the cider or wine (it may well bubble and spit a bit) and give everything a good toss before returning the pan to the oven.

4. When the mussels and clams have popped open, discard any that haven't, take the pan out of the oven and stir in the butter, the herbs and the spinach. Finally, squeeze the juice from the lime over the top and taste before seasoning as it will likely be salty enough. Serve with bread and share with friends.

> Tips
>
> If you haven't got any booze, use decent chicken or fish stock but compensate for the lack of acidity with an extra squeeze of citrus.

Baked Eggs

Breakfast. Lunch. Dinner. Baked eggs are always a hit. Featuring aromatic flavours of sage and thyme.

Prep Time
2 mins

Cook Time
5 mins

Serves
3–4

120ml (4fl oz) olive oil
3 or 4 eggs
Handful of sage leaves
A few sprigs of thyme
Flaky sea salt and freshly ground
  black pepper
Crusty bread, to serve

1. Preheat your pizza oven to 400°C (750°F) (stone floor temperature).
2. Split the oil between three or four small baking dishes and place in the oven for 2–3 minutes until shimmering, then crack an egg into each dish and scatter over the herbs.
3. Place back in the oven for 30 seconds until the white is just set and serve with crusty bread and a good pinch of salt and pepper.

Roasted Vegetables

Simplicity at its best. The high temperature of live-fire cooking brings out unmissable flavours and textures. You'll never want to cook veg another way again.

Prep Time
5 mins

Cook Time
10 mins

Serves
4–6

---

3 courgettes (zucchini), halved
300g (10.5oz) tomatoes (any variety)
200g (7oz) asparagus, woody bases removed
3 tbsp olive oil
A few sprigs of rosemary, leaves removed and finely chopped
A few sprigs of thyme
A few sprigs of oregano
Flaky sea salt and freshly ground black pepper

1. Preheat your pizza oven to 350°C (660°F) (stone floor temperature) with a medium flame and place a baking tray in the oven to heat up for 5 minutes.
2. Cut a shallow crisscross pattern into the courgettes (zucchini), halve any large tomatoes, then gently toss the vegetables in a large bowl with the oil, rosemary and a good pinch each of salt and pepper.
3. Add the vegetables to the tray, holding back any cherry tomatoes, if using, then place in the oven for 3–4 minutes. Nestle in the cherry tomatoes and bake for a few minutes more until the veg is caramelised with a beautiful golden colour.
4. Serve with a final sprinkle of flaky salt and the fresh thyme and oregano.

Baked Potatoes

A British classic. A great side or served as a main, you can pop them onto the embers of your wood fire to cook and not waste a second.

Prep Time
5 mins

Cook Time
45 mins–1 hour

Serves
4

---

4 medium baking potatoes (King
   Edward or Desiree)
38g (1.3oz) butter
Flaky sea salt and freshly ground
   black pepper

1. Heat your pizza oven to 190°C (375°F) (stone floor temperature) and make sure you have a good amount of embers left in the oven.
2. Spike each potato all over with a fork, rub 1 teaspoon of butter onto each potato and sprinkle with flaky salt.
3. Individually wrap the potatoes in two layers of foil, then nestle the potatoes into the embers and cook for 45 minutes to 1 hour, turning the potatoes a few times until they are soft throughout and topping up the fuel to keep the heat steady.
4. Carefully peel back the foil and place on the floor of the oven to crisp up before cutting open and topping with the remaining butter and some salt and pepper.

Missy's Fire-roasted Fennel

Award-winning New York chef, Missy Robbins, rarely lets anyone in on how she creates her mind-blowing dishes. Out of the famed Lilia kitchen and into your garden, try her Fire-roasted Fennel as a side or as the main itself.

Prep Time
5 mins

Cook Time
12 mins

Serves
4–6

---

3 fennel bulbs
4 tbsp olive oil
2 tbsp Kosher or coarse sea salt
Pared peel from 1 lemon, cut into
   large slices
5 sprigs of thyme
25g (0.9oz) Parmigiano Reggiano
½ tbsp fennel pollen
2 tbsp aged balsamic vinegar
Freshly ground black pepper

1. Preheat your pizza oven to 350°C (660°F) (stone floor temperature).
2. Cut the fennel into 5mm (¼in)-thick slices, toss with the olive oil and salt, then spread in a single layer on a large baking tray.
3. Add some black pepper, the lemon peel slices and the sprigs of thyme and roast in the oven for about 10 minutes, turning the tray a few times, until the fennel begins to caramelise, then remove from the oven and remove the lemon peel and thyme.
4. Grate the Parmigiano Reggiano over the top, then place back in the oven for 1–2 minutes until the cheese starts to crisp and brown.
5. Sprinkle the fennel pollen over the top, followed by a drizzle of balsamic vinegar, then serve.

Tapas

One of Tom Gozney's favourite things to cook in a pizza oven. Fun, vibrant and great for sharing.

Tiger Prawns with Garlic & Parsley

Prep Time	Cook Time	Serves
5 mins	5 mins	4–6

20 raw tiger prawns,
  head and shell on
3 tbsp olive oil
3 garlic cloves, thinly sliced
Small bunch of parsley,
  roughly chopped
1 lemon, halved
Flaky sea salt

1. Heat your pizza oven to 250°C (480°F) (stone floor temperature) with a cast-iron pan inside, making sure there's a medium flame.
2. Toss the prawns with the olive oil and a good pinch of salt, then tip them into the hot cast-iron pan and cook in the oven, near the heat source, for 3–4 minutes before adding the garlic.
3. Give everything a stir and cook for a minute or two more until the prawns are all beautifully pink.
4. Scatter the chopped parsley over the prawns and squeeze over some lemon juice before serving.

Roast Almonds

Prep Time	Cook Time	Serves
2 mins	10 mins	4–6

225g (7.9oz) blanched almonds
$\frac{1}{2}$ egg white
$\frac{1}{2}$ tsp smoked paprika
$\frac{1}{8}$ tsp chilli powder
$\frac{1}{4}$ tsp brown sugar
Smoked flaky sea salt

1. Preheat your pizza oven to 200°C (390°F) (stone floor temperature).
2. Mix the almonds with the egg white, then stir in the smoked paprika, chilli powder and sugar and mix well until the almonds are all coated.
3. Spread the almonds out on a baking tray in a single layer and cook in the oven for about 10 minutes, mixing halfway through, until they are golden brown.
4. Sprinkle over some smoked salt and leave to cool a little before serving or leave to cool completely before storing in an airtight container for up to 2 weeks.

Tapas

Padron Peppers

Prep Time	Cook Time	Serves
1 min	5 mins	4–6

300g (10.5oz) padron peppers
2 tbsp extra virgin olive oil
Flaky sea salt

1. Preheat your pizza oven to 250°C (480°F) (stone floor temperature), make sure there's a medium flame and place a cast-iron pan in the oven to heat up.
2. Toss the peppers with the olive oil, then add to the hot pan and cook for 4–5 minutes, tossing the pan occasionally, until the peppers have softened a little and are charred.
3. Remove the pan from the oven, then immediately season the peppers with a good pinch of flaky salt.

Chorizo in Cider

Prep Time	Cook Time	Serves
2 mins	15 mins	4–6

225g (8oz) chorizo, thickly
   sliced
100ml (3.4fl oz) dry cider

1. Preheat your pizza oven to 250°C (480°F) (stone floor temperature) and make sure there's a medium flame.
2. Add the chorizo to a small cast-iron pan and place it in the oven, furthest from the heat source, for about 5 minutes until the chorizo has released a delicious red oil and started to crisp up.
3. Turn the chorizo pieces over, pour in the cider and place back in the oven for about 10 minutes, keeping an eye on the chorizo so it doesn't catch. Remove from the oven when the chorizo is crisp and the cider is syrupy. Serve with big hunks of baguette.

Corn on the Cob

What's outdoor cooking without corn on the cob? And wait until you've tried it cooked with fire. Garlic and herb butter (or harissa butter) melts into the cob making it rich, juicy and full of flavour.

Prep Time
2 mins, plus 15 minutes soaking time

Cook Time
10 mins

Serves
3-6

---

3 sweetcorn cobs
Flaky sea salt

For the garlic and herb butter
100g (3.5oz) unsalted butter,
  softened
2 garlic cloves, crushed
2 tbsp finely chopped soft herbs
  (such as parsley, coriander/
  cilantro, chives etc.)

For the harissa butter
100g (3.5oz) unsalted butter,
  softened
1 tbsp honey
2 tbsp harissa sauce

1. Preheat your pizza oven to 250°C (480°F) (stone floor temperature) with a medium flame.
2. Mix either of the butter ingredients together and set to one side.
3. Pull back the husks of the corn and remove the stringy bits, before placing the corn in a bowl of water for 15 minutes.
4. Place the corn straight on the base of the oven and cook for about 10 minutes, turning them regularly and watching the husks in case they catch fire! Use tongs to hold the corn directly in the flame for a few seconds to encourage some charring if needed.
5. When the corn is soft and charred, remove from the oven, then place on the table and spread your choice of flavoured butter over them and scatter over some flaky salt.

Taleggio Mushrooms

Our take on cheesy mushrooms. Earthy and nutty flavours make this dish a great side at any party.

Prep Time
5 mins

Cook Time
5 mins

Serves
2–4

400g (14oz) mixed mushrooms
(such as shiitake, shimeji,
oyster, maitake)
1 tbsp olive oil
A few sprigs of rosemary,
leaves removed and finely
chopped
100g (3.5oz) taleggio, cubed
Small bunch of parsley, finely
chopped
Flaky sea salt and freshly ground
black pepper

1. Preheat your pizza oven to 300°C (570°F) (stone floor temperature) with a medium flame and place a baking dish or cast-iron pan in the oven to heat up.
2. Toss the mushrooms with the oil, rosemary and a pinch each of salt and pepper, then add to the hot pan.
3. Cook for 4–5 minutes, then dot the taleggio over the mushrooms and cook for a few minutes more until the taleggio has melted a little and the mushrooms have turned golden. Remove from the oven and top with the finely chopped parsley, finishing with a little more salt and pepper.

Roasted Fruit

The only dessert in the book. That says something. We love these roasted fruit recipes. They're all great served with a dollop of ice cream.

Roasted Strawberries

Prep Time	Cook Time	Serves
5 mins	10-15 mins	4-6

400g (14oz) strawberries
1 tbsp black peppercorns, crushed
1 tbsp extra virgin olive oil
1-2 tbsp golden caster (superfine) sugar
2 vanilla bean pods

1. Preheat your pizza oven to 250–300°C (480-570°F) (stone floor temperature) with a medium flame.
2. Place the strawberries on a baking tray and toss with the black pepper, olive oil and sugar.
3. Slice the vanilla pods in half lengthways, leave the tops attached, and nestle them into the strawberries. Roast in the oven for 10–15 minutes, stirring them halfway through, until they have softened and a few have turned soft and syrupy, then remove and leave to cool a little.

Roasted Peaches

Prep Time	Cook Time	Serves
5 mins	15 mins	4-6

4 peaches
2 tbsp honey
1 tbsp extra virgin olive oil
Leaves from a small bunch of lemon thyme

1. Preheat your pizza oven to 250–300°C (480-570°F) (stone floor temperature) with a medium flame.
2. Halve and destone the peaches and place them cut side up in a baking dish or cast-iron pan. Drizzle over the honey and olive oil, then bake in the oven for 15 minutes until caramelised and slightly softened. Remove from the oven and toss over some lemon thyme leaves before serving.

Roasted Pears

Prep Time	Cook Time	Serves
5 mins	15 mins	4-6

4 pears
1 tbsp extra virgin olive oil
½ tsp ground cinnamon
1 tbsp maple syrup
45g (1.6oz) walnuts, roughly chopped

1. Preheat your pizza oven to 250–300°C (480-570°F) (stone floor temperature) with a medium flame.
2. Quarter the pears and spoon out the cores before placing them in a baking dish or cast-iron pan.
3. Drizzle over the olive oil, cinnamon and maple syrup, then bake in the oven for 15 minutes. Add the walnuts halfway through cooking, then return to the oven until the pears are caramelised and slightly softened.

237

Index

Index

Contributors

Adam Atkins
St. Albans, UK

The Gozney OG, hip-hop loving, pizza peddler. Adam's Gozney journey started back in 2016, when he left his delivery job and decided to turn his hobby of making pizzas into his business 'Peddling Pizza'. He strapped Roccboxes on to his bike and trailer and started serving Neapolitan pizzas at the local market in his hometown St Albans (UK). Since then, he's perfected his craft and upgraded to a Chevy American van, which won best-looking food truck at British Street Food 2022 Awards. Over the years Adam has become an inspiration for others investing in building their own businesses and is always supporting them with advice, as well as getting hands on at pizza classes. If you pop to St Albans, you'll find Adam blasting out hip hop from his van, repping his latest sneaker collection addition.

Jhy Coulter
Kansas City, Missouri, USA

From winning her first Roccbox in a Gozney x Matty Matheson Instagram competition back in 2019 to owning one of Kansas City's coolest new pop-ups, Jhy has an incredible story to tell. Gaining her skills through working pizza kitchens during college, Jhy created Devoured Pop Up in Kansas City, MO. Three years later, Devoured is growing and looking to become a brick-and-mortar store soon.

Feng Chen
Bangkok, Thailand

On a small balcony in Bangkok, Thailand, you'll find some of the most beautiful pizzas being crafted by Feng Chen. What started as a personal challenge of making 100 pizzas developed into a passion and a personal style and expression of pizza making. Feng's built a reputation for creating perfect leopard-spotted pizza crusts.

Jon Shook & Vinny Dotolo
Los Angeles, California, USA

Jon and Vinny are LA's favourite duo and the cool kids of culinary. With their bold flavours, playful attitude, and unapologetic love of carbs, they're the masterminds behind some of the best food you'll ever try. Experimenting with innovative twists on classic comfort food, they've become renowned for restaurants such as Jon & Vinny's and Son of a Gun. They've created a community around their restaurants, sharing their passion for hospitality, and their genuine love of their customers, making sure everyone feels welcome and leaves happy. Jon and Vinny are the kind of chefs who remind you why you fell in love with food in the first place.

Ines Barlerin Glaser
Venice, California, USA

Ines is a badass pizza chef based in Venice, California, known for throwing the best pizza parties, catering private events, and teaching people how to create pro pies with her pop-up business Lupa Cotta.

Brad Leone
Connecticut, USA

Brad brings the fun to cooking with fire. Born and raised in New Jersey, Brad grew up hunting, fishing and immersing himself in nature, which is where his love of food and cooking in the wild began. He started out in the test kitchen at Bon Appetit and worked his way to become the host of his own channel on YouTube with a cult following for his shows 'Makin' It' and 'Local Legends.' With his infectious laugh and incredible sense of humour, it's hard not to follow along his recipes.

Luis Perez
Rochester, New York, USA

Buying a Roccbox kickstarted Luis Perez's street pizza business back in 2016, serving pizza from his 3-wheeled Piaggio Ape van in Rochester, NY. Since then, Luis opened his own slice shop and has a loyal customer base coming back week after week for their pizza fix. Luis was not only a guest chef but a main contributor to our pizza recipe development.

Frank Pinello
Brooklyn, New York, USA

Frank's a legend in New York city's pizza scene. As the host of 'The Pizza Show' on Vice and the owner of Best Pizza, he's become a household name among pizza aficionados. He's travelled all over the world in search of the perfect slice, but he always comes back to his roots in New York. Frank's friendly, lovable demeanour makes him a pleasure to hang out and cook with.

Richard Preston
Christchruch, Dorset, UK

Better known as Richie P., Gozney's own Content Director and resident pizza maker. What started out as a job making all the dough before video shoots has turned into a love affair for the UK native. A professional drummer as well as photographer: one of Gozney's longest-running team members.

Missy Robbins
New York, USA

Missy has a passion for Italian cuisine that knows no bounds. Her culinary journey has taken her from the streets of NYC to the landscapes of Tuscany, resulting in the most extraordinary creations and flavours using only the very best quality ingredients. Missy owns two Italian restaurants in Williamsburg, Brooklyn, Lilia and Misi, which opened in 2016 and 2018 respectively. She reigns supreme among the culinary elite.

Chris Roberts
Wales, United Kingdom

Surrounded by the Welsh countryside, the place he calls home, or out on the streets of NYC, Chris Roberts aka 'Flamebaster' fires up everything from meat and fish to flat breads and vegetables. Pairing his big personality with big flavours.

Lee Tiernan
London, UK

The king of rock-and-roll and head-bangingly good food. As the owner and head chef of F.K.A.B.A.M. in his hometown London, Lee has become a cult hero among foodies and metalheads. He's known for his unconventional flavour combinations (think lamb offal with Korean chili paste and squid ink flatbreads), his love of all things spicy, and his adventurous nature of experimenting with techniques like smoking, grilling and fermenting. Not to mention firing up the majority of his dishes in his Warrior-themed Gozney commercial oven. Lee's not afraid to push the boundaries of what's possible.

Daniele Uditi
Los Angeles, California, USA

Daniele Uditi is LA's fun-loving Italian pizzaiolo and head chef at Pizzana, who's gained global recognition for his pizza skills and hosting his own TV show 'Best in Dough'. He learnt his craft growing up in Naples, Italy, and since his arrival to LA back in 2010 has become famous for his signature 'slow dough' Neo-Neapolitan pizzas, with a cult following from celebrities and pizza lovers across the world.

Acknowledgements

There are so many people that I am grateful for, who have left imprints on my journey, too many to fit on one page.

Thank you to the entire Gozney family, those at headquarters, our advocates and partners. You are the driving force behind the business bringing the brand and my vision to life in so many new and exciting ways.

Thank you to our amazing community of chefs and home cooks. You inspire us on a daily basis. Our ovens are built to be used and you give us our lifeblood by doing exactly that.

Thank you to my parents, none of this would have been possible without your unwavering support. Always being there, through my darkest moments and into brighter seasons, never giving up on me. You taught me that anything is possible, that I can achieve anything I set my mind to, and to believe in myself when others don't. Whether fighting addiction or pursuing my vision to build a global brand, thank you for always believing in me and for being my biggest supporters.

To my wife, Laura, my rock, best friend, and business partner. You're the unsung hero in the Gozney growth journey. From packing parcels in the freezing cold, dusty, wet warehouse in the beginning, to learning how to run finance, operations, sales, marketing, and everything else that the business needed from us. You built this brand with me and continue to shape so much of its future whilst also being an incredible mum to our babies. Love you babe. Thank you.

Finally, Tigger, Eden, Seven anything is possible, LFG.

- Tom

Concept development & principal photography
Richard Preston

Concept and Creative Direction, Design
Chatham Baker

Recipe development and styling
Pippa Leon

Styling
Faye Wears

Recipe development
Luis Perez

Graphic Design
Nita Elinski

Illustration
DOOOM

Support copywriting
Laura Gozney, Caitlin Fogarty, Richard Preston, Chatham Baker

Additional contributors
Alex Heckford, Laura Booth, Rick Bannister

Photography by:
Richard Preston
Przemek Przystup
Tal Roberts
Mark Welsh
Sian Angharad
Apinut Sinra / Feng Chen
Billy Watts
Julian Martin
Lindsey Childs
John Barton
Yasmin Mund
Willie Woodward
John Deptulski - Studio H
James Williams
Rich 'Lil BLind' Hull
Jack Newton
Matthew Rattew

Thank you

Laura Gozney / Colin Gozney / Linda Gozney / Therese Plastow / Richard Plastow / Fay Lai / Geoff Lai / Maria Gozney / Scarlett Lai / Reeve Lai / Maxine Mincham / Ryan Mincham / Riley Mincham / Harper Mincham

The Gozney Pizza Collective / The Gozney Pizza Club / Missy Robbins / Adam Atkins / Brad Leone / Chris Bianco / Danny Bowien / Eric Wareheim / Frank Pinello / Jon Shook & Vinny Dotolo / Joshua Weissman / Lee Tiernan / Matty Matheson / Sean Feeney / Austin Smith / Brad Carter / Brianna Cope / Bryce Miller / Candice Brown / Chris Roberts / Chrissy Tracey / Christian Petroni / Courtney Storer / Daniele Uditi / David Lee / Dean Petty / Drew Huston / Edu Lavandeira / Farideh Sadeghin / Feng Chen / Florian Deffte / Ian Niklaus / Ines Barlerin Glaser / Isobel Little / Jeremy Charles / Jessica Nguyen / Jhy Coulter / Joel Bennetts / John Chantarsarak / Juan G Perez / Karan Gokani / Luis Perez / Luke Marrazzi / Luke Powell / Philli Armitage Mattin / Rasheed Philips / Rene Strgar / Richard Bertinet / Mark Welsh / Jon Hetchkopf / Tal Roberts / Jon Ray / Sage Cattabriga-Alosa / Salim Gafayri / Sarah Glover / Thom Bateman / Thuy Pham / Tony Scardino / Willie Woodward / Yadin Nicol / Charlotte Hemmings / Millie van Grutten / Lydia Good / India Baker

Adrian Apanowicz / Alan Xu / Alex Heckford / Alice Zhang / Ally Dykman / Amy Baker / Andrew Nagel Smith / Androulla Van Graan / Angelina Krankenedl / Antony Lyall / April Ding / Arek Flak / Arthur Brunetti / Arturo Lozano Aparicio / Ashley Smith / Ashlie Garr / Austin Bushman / Becky Smart / Bethany Holmes / Brian Skorupski / Brittany Schuhmacher / Brooke Gulian / Caitlin Fogarty / Calvert Schaefer / Casey Conway / Chatham Baker / Chloe Massiah / Chris Darrah / Chris Fu / Chris Gengaro / Chris Nelson / Chris Springer / Christopher Mackanich / Clare O'Brien / Claudia Marsh / Dan Madura / Dariusz Galazewski / David Moorhouse / Daylen Bushman / Denny Bruce / Devin Soisson / Dustin Joyce / Gemma Almeida / George Harrod / Hannah Rendel / Hubert Trafny / Jack Cawdery / Jack Simpson / Jade Heathman / James Kirk / Jeff Carpenter / Jenna Perez / Jenny Barnard / Jim Isome / Jonathan Kantor / Jordan Jones / Joshua Peterson / Josh Tunstill / Julie Kingrey / Justin Sell / Kacey Blackner / Ken Hou / Kiara Isted / Kina Qi / Kirsty Tansey / Kyle Kennedy / Lance Meller / Laura Booth / Lauren Davis / Lauren Marsh / Lemon Jin / Leo Wang / Linda Butler / Lucy Luvaglia / Mariana Guillot / Mark Cannings / Mark Davis / Mark Kosiba / Marc Schechter / Martin Dexter / Matt Underwood / Matthew Rattew / Megan Lee / Michael Burridge / Michael Davis / Michael Zhu / Michal Klapsa / Nathan Miceli / Nicole Tannarome / Nita Elinski / Oliver Perretta / Olivia Sargeant/ Oluwaseyi (Seyi) Oso / Owen Feeney / Patrick Welton / Paul Klauser / Paul Tanu / Paula Guillot / Polly Connolly / Przemek Pryzstup / Reece Marshallsay / Richard Bannister / Richard Preston / Rita Poluchuck / Rob Mclennand / Robin Sun / Roxanne Cooper-Costello / Russell Gibb / Ryan Breeze / Ryan Mazzie / Sarah Metzger / Scott Riley / Simon Henderson / Steve Dong / Tyler Jones / Victoria Edwards / Vincent Yang / Yve Kuefner

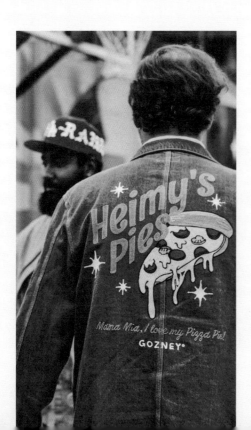